WALKS FOR ALL AGES
CHESHIRE

WALKS FOR ALL AGES

CHESHIRE

NEIL BURGESS

BRADWELL
BOOKS

Published by Bradwell Books
9 Orgreave Close Sheffield S13 9NP
Email: books@bradwellbooks.co.uk

British Library Cataloguing in Publication Data: a catalogue record for this book is available from the British Library.

1st Edition

ISBN: 9781910551523

Print: Gomer Press, Llandysul, Ceredigion SA44 4JL

Design by: Andrew Caffrey

Typesetting by: Mark Titterton

Photographs: The author

Maps: Contain Ordnance Survey data
© Crown copyright and database right 2016

Ordnance Survey licence number 100039353

The information in this book has been produced in good faith and is intended as a general guide. Bradwell Books and its authors have made all reasonable efforts to ensure that the details are correct at the time of publication. Bradwell Books and the author cannot accept any responsibility for any changes that have taken place subsequent to the book being published. It is the responsibility of individuals undertaking any of the walks listed in this publication to exercise due care and consideration for the health and wellbeing of each other in the party. Particular care should be taken if you are inexperienced. The walks in this book are not especially strenuous but individuals taking part should ensure they are fit and able to complete the walk before setting off.

CONTENTS

Walks are listed in order of exertion, easiest first

WHITHER CHESHIRE

MENTION CHESHIRE TO MANY PEOPLE AND THEY'LL PROBABLY THINK OF A LUSH, GRASSY COUNTRYSIDE WHERE THE HALF-TIMBERED HOUSES MATCH THE BLACK-AND-WHITE CATTLE. A LAND OF PRETTY VILLAGES AND FARMS WHERE CHESHIRE CHEESE MEETS THE LIGHT OF DAY; A WEB OF COUNTRY LANES THREADING A FLAT, FERTILE PLAIN WHERE THE CHESHIRE SET AND THE 'FOOTBALLER BELT' SOUTH OF MANCHESTER ARE FAMILIAR STEREOTYPES.

Let's smash that vision. It is indeed a bucolic scene that often greets the eye, but this partners an endlessly intriguing heritage and history that will tantalise and richly reward the curious visitor. This is one of the oldest counties in the realm, stretching from the atmospheric coastal sea-marshes of The Wirral's Dee Estuary in the west to the rippling hills and wild moors of the east, where lie some of England's highest pubs within the fringe of the country's first National Park, the Peak District. In between, remnants of Norman forests hide mysterious meres and winding gorges, whilst castles, country houses and landed estates generously dapple the landscape.

Mining for copper, salt and coal amongst other minerals has bequeathed a remarkable range of locations to explore, whilst stone quarrying cleaves the gritstone edges of the eastern fringe. Canals thread the countryside, linking towns whose development was generated by industries such as silk weaving and cotton spinning. The Industrial Revolution grew up here, bequeathing a glorious mix of deeply rural landscapes and engaging technological inventiveness to track down.

The walks included in this book take full advantage of such diversity. From the Roman and medieval townscape of fabulous Chester to the ghostly hillforts of the county's sandstone spine; from planned industrial communities to tranquil hamlets hidden along no-through-roads; from astonishing viewpoints to absorbing backwaters, a generous network of footpaths, tracks and lanes opens up a memorable bag of destinations awaiting your discovery. Cheshire truly is a county of the unexpected.

FARNDON AND HOLT

WALK ACROSS A NATIONAL FRONTIER TO CASTLE RUINS AND A HAUNTED BRIDGE

In the south-west of Cheshire, the River Dee is the border between England and Wales. The river makes a tortuous route through dozens of tight bends across a relatively flat countryside, fringed to the west by the shadowy Clwydian Range of shapely hills beyond Wrexham. The area is dotted with small towns and villages with a heritage going back millennia; this short and easy walk links two of these, one each side of the national boundary in these northern Welsh Marches.

The walk commences on the English side of the Dee at Farndon. The ancient sandstone bridge across the river here is little altered since medieval times. It's still just wide enough for a generous cart, whilst its ruby red cutwaters slice into the Dee's vigorous flow as they have for over 700 years. Spookily, this atmospheric bridge is said to  be haunted. The young sons of the Welsh leader Madog ap Gruffydd were put in the guardianship of the powerful Norman Marcher Lord Roger Mortimer. Seizing his chance to promote his campaign for a larger power base, Mortimer is said to have had the boys drowned by flinging them in sacks off the bridge here. Their screams are claimed to be occasionally heard rising from beneath the bridge at the dead of night.

The small town itself is curled around the sandstone spur on which stands Farndon's medieval church, built about the same time as the bridge. Lanes and paths make exploring the place a pleasant diversion before falling back to the riverside. Somewhere here in AD 924 the King of Wessex, Edward the Elder, son of Alfred the Great, was killed in a skirmish with Welsh forces and Mercian rebels. It's much more peaceful hereabouts nowadays, although crossing the river into Wales now entails a short stretch beside the busy main road on the modern bypass bridge.

Tranquillity soon returns as the way heads north to riverside meadows at Holt, where a sandstone bluff is capped by the ruins of Holt Castle. This was built for Edward the First, securing his recent conquest of much of North Wales, and entrusted to the powerful baron John de Warrene. The compact town of Holt grew up to serve it. The fortress was destroyed in Owain Glyndŵr's revolt in 1400, then rebuilt before eventually being made ruinous at the end of the Civil War in about 1650, having been the last castle in the north of Wales to fall to the Parliamentary side after a major skirmish. Stones from the castle were used to build new houses in the town; some was boated downstream to be used in the huge mansion house being built for the influential Grosvenor family near Chester.

THE BASICS

Distance: 2½ miles / 4km

Gradient: Several gradual ascents and descents

Severity: Easy

Approx. time to walk: 1½ hours

Stiles: One, plus handgates and some steps

Map: OS Explorer 257 (Crewe and Nantwich)

Path description: Riverside paths, village lanes, short main road section

Start point: Farndon (GR SJ 412545)

Parking: Car park (free) beside Farndon Bridge (CH3 6PU)

Dog friendly: On leads where appropriate

Public toilets: Holt

Nearest refreshment: Pubs and cafés in Farndon and Holt

FARNDON AND HOLT WALK

1. Turn right uphill from the car park entrance. The river here, still navigable today, enabled monks at an early monastery to trade with the outside world. The circular churchyard wall suggests a very early monastic foundation existed here. Within metres turn right up the walled track to reach a crossways. Go left to reach the main road. Turn uphill and pass by The Farndon Inn. Just beyond, turn right on Church Street to reach the churchyard gates. Take time to visit St Chad's Church before returning to Church Street and heading right, past the village hall.

2. Remain with the winding back lane until a point just before regaining the main road. Here; turn right on Old Lane to reach a path junction at a bend in 150 metres. Fork right and drop down steps to find the Dee; turn upstream. The good path slinks past low cliffs and then heads through riverside meadows and fields via a stile and kissing gate to reach the bypass bridge.

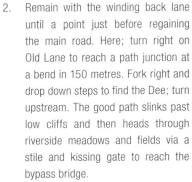

3. Immediately before the bridge, climb the metal steps up onto the main road. Cross the bridge and look for similar steps down. Turn right; slip left onto the tarred lane, then use the handgate into riverside pastures, this time heading downstream, presently reaching Holt Castle. A series of boards detail the site's history.

4. Join the continuing path behind the information board nearest the river.

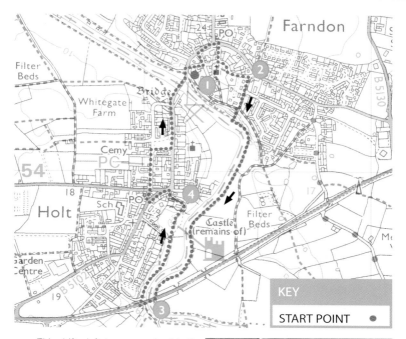

This drifts left to emerge beside the village's former endowed school. Beyond, slip left to reach the little town square and medieval cross. Well-placed information boards reveal the area's heritage. Look for Cross Street and head along this to reach the village green. Turn right and walk to the church, another St Chad's, snuggled behind the Peal o' Bells pub. The church was used during the Civil War to imprison Royalist prisoners in this Commonwealth town. There are musket ball holes in evidence in the wall near the ancient font inside the building.

Return to the main road and turn right to follow it through to cross the medieval bridge. It dates from around 1345 and once had a chapel-tower halfway across. From a wharf in this area in Roman times, tiles made in a works at the edge of Holt were moved by boat to Chester.

WHITEGATE AND NUNSMERE

EXPLORE HEATHLAND, INDUSTRIAL HERITAGE, COOL WOODS
AND TREE-HIDDEN LAKES NEAR AN IMMENSE TREE NURSERY

One area of the heart of Cheshire is characterised by drifts of woodland; areas of warm gorsey heath; small, sharply cut little valleys and great sheets of water. This miniature lakeland largely didn't exist a century ago; it owes its current landscape to the demands of industry and the construction sector.

Between Winsford, Delamere and Northwich a series of vast sand quarries has been delved into the gently undulating countryside. This area of the Cheshire Plain was at the fringe of the huge ice-sheets which covered much of northern England 15,000 years ago. The copious sands are the remains of rocks crushed by the immense weight and movement of the 2km-thick ice-sheet and then deposited under the ice and laid down in thick beds. The advent of concrete as a building material after the Great War saw the need for huge amounts of sand to be used in the mix. Geologists identified these Cheshire deposits as ideal; the huge pits passed on this walk are the result.

They're not industrial eyesores, however. Most are now long disused and have been landscaped, or reclaimed naturally over the years. Woodland-fringed, with colourful water-plants, islets and boggy fringes, they're the perfect habitat for a wide variety of birds, dragonflies and other water specialists.

This level, easy walk passes some of these woodland waters, approaching via the trackbed of an old railway that was built to transport salt from Cheshire's famous salt mines near Winsford. The Whitegate Way is now a tranquil recreational trail linking heath and woodland. Opened in 1870, the line finally closed in 1968. Whitegate Station, base for this walk, closed as long ago as 1931.

The walk heads for Newchurch Common. This was at the heart of a vast 5,000-acre estate held by the great Abbey at Vale Royal, just two miles away beyond Whitegate village. This was one of the largest Cistercian Houses in the country; founded by Prince Edward – later King Edward I – as thanks to God for his rescue from a shipwreck. Destroyed by Henry VIII, its lands passed to the Cholmondeley family, who held them for centuries. Many of the grand country houses dotted amidst these favoured Cheshire acres were built as homes for family members in Georgian and Victorian times. Local talk suggests that, during the Second War, King George VI and Queen Elizabeth escaped the London Blitz to spend a rare few days in peace at one of these secluded Cheshire retreats.

Other wartime guests also stayed in the area. The small estate of smart bungalows passed late in the walk are built on the site of Marton Residential Camp. This was used by child evacuees escaping the bombing of Liverpool Docks from 1940 onwards.

THE BASICS

Distance: 4½ miles / 7.2km

Gradient: Virtually level throughout

Severity: Easy

Approx. time to walk: 2½ hours

Stiles: None; several handgates

Map: OS Explorer 267 (Northwich and Delamere Forest)

Path description: Old railway, tarred lanes, woodland and heath paths

Start point: Whitegate Old Station (GR SJ 615679)

Parking: Old Station Car Park (free) (CW7 2QE)

Dog friendly: On leads where appropriate

Public toilets: At start

Nearest refreshment: Pub at Foxwist Green within 1 mile

1. Leave the car parking area, pass under the road bridge and head off up the old track. In 500 metres you'll reach wooden stables up on your left and railings protruding onto the track. Look for the path on your right, leaving the old trackbed to join a paddock-edge path through further gates to reach a tarred lane. Turn left and follow it to and past a gated semi-barrier across the lane.

2. In another 150 metres keep eyes peeled for a waymarked wooden fingerpost indicating a path to the left. Turn along this, which winds through scrubby birchwoods to approach the lip of one of the flooded pits here. Now the path loops clockwise around the water in a strand of trees before re-emerging onto the now-rougher lane by an anglers' car park. Go left and walk it for 1km, another lake now to your right. Beyond the secluded farm cottage it becomes a sandy track.

3. The track becomes tarred at the entrance to a scouting activity centre. Look left for the 'Restricted Byway' signed past the barrier and join this. You'll presently cross a bridge over the Whitegate Way; continue ahead past the car park on the forestry track, from which views presently reveal the large lake of Nunsmere through the trees on your right. There's a large country house hotel visible here; Nunsmere Hall was built in 1900 for shipping company magnate Sir Aubrey Brocklebank. He was one of the designers of the transatlantic liner *Queen Mary*. The track becomes hard-surfaced again.

4. Where the track bends sharply right, take the dirt path directly left, which soon comes to run beside fenced pine and birch woods fringing an area of lowland heath on your left. This can be a great place for birds like buzzards and short-eared owls. Simply trace this path – popular with horse-riders, too – to reach the gated entrance to the Forestry Commission tree nursery of Abbots Moss, where an incredible 14 million plants are cultivated each year. Turn right; then go immediately left along the hard-surfaced fenced track between areas of infant trees. At the end pass a barrier and advance along the oak-lined green track.

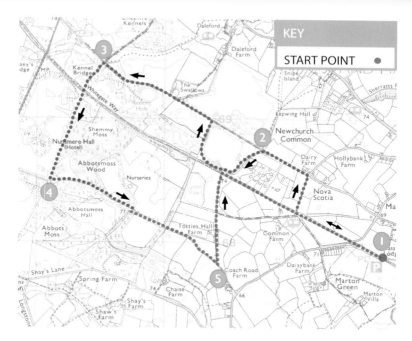

5. In 450 metres this old lane reaches a junction with a gravelled farm driveway. Turn left and walk towards the houses. Go through the waymarked wooden gate and ahead to slip beside Totties Hall Farmhouse. Go ahead via gates past the barns and yard, keeping ahead to a wooded strip fringing a rough lane. Cross ahead-left onto a continuing fenced path, presently reaching a gate onto the Whitegate Way. Turn right back to base; off to your left are the bungalows on the site of the former evacuee camp; it later became a residential school owned by Northumberland County Council.

DEE ESTUARY

Walk the atmospheric Deeside marshes to ghosts of industry with fabulous views to the Welsh hills

Few people realise that Cheshire has a coastal strip. Until 1974 it was considerably greater in extent and covered the entire Wirral coastline; nowadays it's just the southern end of the land between the Dee and Mersey Estuaries that is still part of the county.

But what an intriguing area this is. A string of villages spread along the northern/eastern bank of the Dee, each one with a fascinating history and much to explore. This walk saunters between two of these settlements at the very edge of Cheshire, discovering lots of history and heritage along the way. An added bonus is the glorious view across the widening Dee Estuary to the green hills of Flintshire beyond the far bank. Take some binoculars with you!

The walk is based on the RSPB Reserve of Gayton Sands, immediately north of the waterside village of Parkgate. This is one of the charity's several interlinked sites along the seamarshes which stretch from the Cheshire shore well out into the estuary. It's also one of the best places to view a wide variety of rare birds from the comparative comfort of the esplanade. The star species here in winter is the extremely rare hen harrier, whilst long and short-eared owls can be regularly seen quartering the marshes. The bird used as the RSPB logo, the avocet, arrives for the spring, whilst little egrets are now a common sight.

The walk heads south along Parkgate's promenade. This appealing village was for many years the port for Chester. Silting upstream meant that Chester itself became landlocked by the 1600s, so a series of quays and docks were developed downstream, moving nearer the sea as further silting occurred. Parkgate's busiest time was from the 1720s, when the packet boats to Ireland loaded here. It's said that the composer Handel landed here when returning from the premier of his *Messiah* in Dublin. The village later became a favoured bathing resort before silting created the immense marshes which now front the promenade.

Beyond Parkgate the way traces a route beside huge reedbeds before skirting marsh-edge pastures to find remnants of the little-known West Cheshire Coalfield. A string of small collieries worked seams way out beneath the estuary; some moving coal by undersea canals before sending it by mineral railway or coastal ships. Small quays moulder in the reeds, whilst that at Little Neston is a marvellous place to linger and explore – The Harp Inn here has fascinating photos and artefacts.

Turning inland, the route presently crosses an old mineral line before joining the Wirral Way. This recreational footpath – the first Country Park in Britain (1973) – uses the trackbed of the old line to West Kirby to return to Gayton.

THE BASICS

Distance: 5 miles / 8km

Gradient: Largely level

Severity: Easy

Approx. time to walk: 2½ to 3 hours

Stiles: Two, plus hand gates

Map: OS Explorer 266 (Wirral and Chester)

Path description: Old railway, roads and lanes, dirt paths

Start point: Parkgate (GR SJ 284778)

Parking: Wirral Way/RSPB car park at Parkgate (free), look for the sign at The Boat House pub at the north end of Parkgate promenade (CH64 6RN)

Dog friendly: On leads where appropriate

Public toilets: Parkgate

Nearest refreshment: Pubs and cafés in Parkgate; Harp Inn, Little Neston

DEE ESTUARY WALK

1. Return from the car park to pass by The Boat House pub and continue along the promenade here at Parkgate. For much of the time it's a grassy, reedy expanse, held back by the old sea-wall along which you're walking. Higher tides leave pools dotting these sea-edge marshes, whilst very high tides see the water lapping the wall. At any time it's worth keeping an eye out for some of the water birds that make it home.

   The strand of imposing buildings at Parkgate front include the eye-catching Mostyn House School, which closed in 2010 and is now apartments. Where the promenade bends left at The Old Quay pub, keep ahead along South Parade, then continue along the walled path above the foreshore which soon bends left as an enclosed path to reach Manorial Road. Turn right along this; in 150 metres slip ahead on the short path past a barrier, then go ahead on Manorial Road South.

2. At the far end, Old Quay Close, turn right along the wide track, soon reaching the edge of the marshes at a small green. Here turn left (not ahead into the reeds) on the path beside a fence. It's a tranquil passage alongside the estuary; the footpath sticks close to the edge, in places across boardwalk. Past a metal kissing gate, keep ahead across pasture and over two footbridges to reach a worn stone step stile in a wall. Here too are old wharves, once the thriving Little Neston Quay. Mark this place, as it's where the return leg leaves from.

   Initially, keep ahead, soon passing the scrub-covered mounds that are all that's left of Little Neston and Wirral Collieries. When you reach housing, advance to find the Harp Inn. Just past this is Denhall Quay, built in 1791 to export coal mined at Ness Colliery, which stood close to the pub.

3. Retrace your route to use the worn stone step stile by the crumbled quay and turn right on the firm path. Use a kissing gate, then pass another and go over the wide

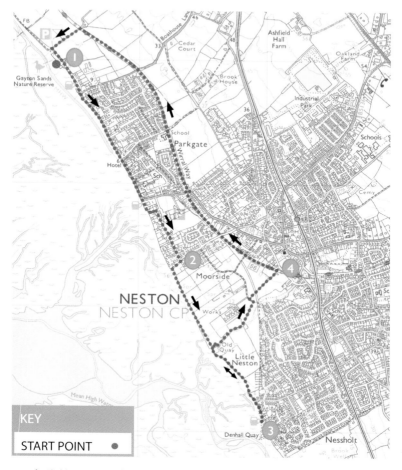

footbridge across a brook. Keep ahead on the wide path; this soon bends left as a hedged way. In 50 metres use the waymarked kissing gate beneath oaks on your right. Take the path ahead-left across the paddock, then cross the old colliery railway trackbed and continue up the left edge of the field to reach another old railway at wooden gates.

4. Turn left on this, which is the Wirral Way footpath. Simply remain with this (either path, hard-surfaced or dirt) for 1km to reach a car park and barrier. Turn right up the main road and cross to rejoin the continuing Wirral Way just before the bend. Stay with this for over 1km to pass beneath an overbridge. At the next overbridge, climb the steps on the right and cross the bridge, joining an old lane that drops to the marsh-edge, with lovely views across to Halkyn Mountain. The car park is to your left.

CHESTER – WALLS AND WATERWAYS

Walk contrasting watersides to and through
Chester's alluring heritage

It must have been an astonishing sight
to residents of the Roman city of Deva.
Beyond the western walls was spread one of
Roman Britain's largest ports. Wharves and
causeways intermingled where goods were
imported and exported – wine from Spain or
olive oil from Libya, Welsh lead, copper and
grain – whilst military craft ferried troops
and livestock from other Irish Sea ports at
places like Caernarfon and Ravenglass.

Fast-forward around a thousand years and
the port was at the heart of the Norman
takeover of the British Isles. It was a vital

lynchpin for the wars against the Welsh Princes in North Wales and also a staging post
for expeditions to Ireland, where the Normans established substantial feudal agricultural
colonies. Chester's racecourse at The Roodee now covers this lost route to the sea.

Whilst this scene is now only in the mind's eye (the port was silting up by the 1350s), other
waterways continue to thrive and prosper at the heart of one of the most historic cities in
the country. For centuries Dee 'flats' (trading barges) used to ply the River Dee between
Bangor (near Wrexham) and Chester; today's traffic is almost entirely recreational, with
pleasure cruises from the quays at the riverside Groves heading upstream towards
Eccleston. It's an interesting way to view the city; viewed across the green meadows of
The Earl's Eye as you drift below the elegant mansions and villas of Boughton.

An equally significant waterway first arrived at the city in the 1770s; a barge canal down
the length of Cheshire that eventually linked up with the national canal network in the south
and the Mersey Estuary at Ellesmere Port to the north. This canal still sweeps around the
fringe of the city centre and provides a memorable walk below the precipitous ramparts of
the city walls. Some of the most challenging locks on the entire canal network drop down
steeply at Northgate to the old canal port developed just outside the Roman walls. It's
worth lingering here to watch the sometimes hair-raising progress of boats up and down
this watery staircase! Although much redeveloped, there's still a boatbuilder's here and
plenty of moorings. The Shropshire Union Canal is now a popular cruising waterway and
the entire stretch is usually bright with colourful narrowboats.

It's the walls which offer a fine and unique prospect of Chester's compact city centre. A circuit of these offers views to the Cathedral, 'The Rows' (two-storey medieval shopping arcades), the Roman amphitheatre and the Victorian promenade of The Groves. Plenty of steps allow frequent diversions to the central lanes, byways and shops spread between the magnificent cathedral and the garland of green parkland above the river.

THE BASICS

Distance: 4¾ miles / 7.6km

Gradient: Largely level, but several lots of steps

Severity: Easy

Approx. time to walk: 3 hours

Stiles: None, several handgates; lots of easy steps around the City Walls

Map: OS Explorer 266 (Wirral and Chester)

Path description: Riverside paths, towpath, city lanes, wall-path

Start point: High Cross, Chester city centre (GR SJ 405663)

Parking: Many car parks in Chester, or use the Park & Ride services from the outskirts

Dog friendly: On leads where appropriate

Public toilets: City centre locations

Nearest refreshment: Ample eating and drinking opportunities

CHESTER
WALLS AND WATERWAYS WALK

1. The route leaves the city centre down Bridge Street, from the High Cross outside St Peter's Church. Keep downhill over the inner ring road to reach Bridgegate. Cross the Old Dee Bridge and take the steps immediately on the left to join a path above the Dee and the weir. This cuts below flats, continuing beneath trees to reach the graceful Queen's Park footbridge.

2. Rise up to the bridge but don't cross it; instead turn left along the nearby Victoria Crescent. In 120 metres fork right (still Victoria Crescent) to the junction. Here cross diagonally-right into St Georges Crescent; keep left on this to pass the end of Edinburgh Way into a short cul-de-sac, Bottoms Lane. The gateway at the end leads onto The Meadows.

3. Follow the hedged pathway ahead to the riverbank. Turn left to walk downstream around the Earl's Eye bend. These meadows were presented to Chester Corporation in 1929 as land for recreational use in perpetuity. Stick with the riverside path to again reach Queen's Park footbridge. This time cross it and go ahead up the steps at the far end. Keep ahead past the ruins of St John's Church, Chester's original cathedral, towards the main road.

4. Turn left to find the pedestrian walkway across the Roman amphitheatre. Beyond, pass under New Bridge and turn immediately

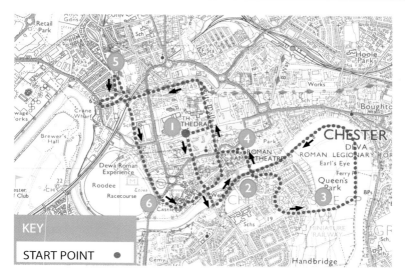

KEY

START POINT ●

back-left up steps onto the walls. Cross the bridge and remain on the walls, over Eastgate Bridge with its ornate clock and then past the Cathedral. Just beyond the Dean's Field Falconry Centre, and before the King's Tower, use the wooden steps (right) down off the walls and drop to the canal towpath. Turn left and walk this deep cutting beneath the walls. Just beyond the high Northgate Bridge are the spectacular locks. From the foot of these follow the canal round to the old covered dock ('Warehouse Workshop').

5. Cross the footbridge, left, over Lock 1; from the nearby doorway turn left along Whipcord Lane beside the lower canal arm. Cross the main road and turn with the canal in front of modern flats. At the end is the ring road, beyond which the canal has a rarely used connection with the River Dee. Turn left along the ring road a few paces, then left up Tower Road. At the junction opposite 'Telford's Warehouse' turn hard-right through bollards. Bear right and up steps onto the walls; turn right to pass the Water Tower. The path soon becomes a pavement above playing fields, then crosses Watergate Bridge to become a promenade above the racecourse.

6. Cross the busy main road at traffic lights, here re-joining the wall-path below the remnants of Chester Castle. This drops to a riverside lane at the university buildings. Within 200 metres re-join the wall-path across Bridgegate, continuing then on the walls above the weir and The Groves promenade. Remain with the wall-path, eventually reaching the Eastgate Clock. Leave the walls and walk past The Grosvenor Hotel to the junction. You're back at the city centre near the High Cross.

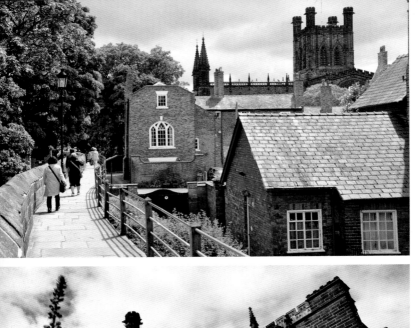

NANTWICH WATERS

A LOOK AT THE TRANSPORT, INDUSTRIAL AND MEDICINAL WATERS IN AND AROUND THIS BEAUTIFUL OLD TOWN

The '*wich*' part of the town's name gives away its genesis as a location where salt was worked many hundreds of years ago. In fact the Romans are known to have tapped the natural brine wells in the area. Past archaeological excavations have revealed a plank tank and lead brine pans nearly 2,000 years old; Roman roads allowed the transportation of this valuable resource all across the Midlands and further afield. The famous Domesday survey of 1086 records salthouses being worked near the river; by the time of Henry VIII the town was, after Chester, the largest and most important in Cheshire.

A dramatic fire in 1583 almost totally destroyed the entire town, with only three buildings of any size surviving. These included the huge St Mary's Church which commands the town centre. The town amply repays a leisurely exploration, with a wealth of buildings resulting from the great rebuilding after the great fire, largely paid for by a national appeal launched by Queen Elizabeth I. Many elegant mansions and villas built for merchants survive. Welsh Row, which features in this walk, is a particularly good survival of this post-medieval period. The town's salt industry lasted until after the Civil War, but declined significantly thereafter due to competition from foreign imports. A further blow came with the development of much larger saltworks and mining at Northwich and Winsford, which Nantwich was unable to match.

In Victorian times the town was re-launched as a health resort, based on the supposed medical properties of the brine wells that still continued to flow. In 1883 outdoor brine baths were created to the north of the town's bridge; these still survive. Around the same period to the south of the town an impressive Georgian hall was much remodelled and extended. Shrewbridge Hall became the Brine Baths Hotel, a medicinal spa with over 50 bedrooms whose patrons took hydropathic cures and medicinal baths. It survived as a hotel until after World War II, when it became a miners' convalescent home, eventually being demolished in 1959.

This walk starts from a lake created in the 1970s in the grounds of the spa hotel. We then meander across to the Shropshire Union Canal towpath, joining this on its progression along a huge embankment above the town. This was completed in 1835, part of an extension of the canal between Chester and Nantwich which had been opened to a wharf north-west of the town in 1779. The two canals met head-on just to the north of the bulky aqueduct where this walk drops down to Welsh Row. From the nearby town centre the River Weaver is accompanied back to the start.

THE BASICS

Distance: 3¼ miles / 5.2km

Gradient: Largely level

Severity: Easy

Approx. time to walk: 2 hours

Stiles: None, around 8 bridgegates; steps at canal

Map: OS Explorer 257 (Crewe and Nantwich)

Path description: Roads, field paths, parkland, towpath

Start point: Nantwich Lake (GR SJ 650514)

Parking: Lakeside car park (free) (CW5 7AE)

Dog friendly: On leads where appropriate

Public toilets: Nantwich

Nearest refreshment: Cafés and pubs in Nantwich centre

NANTWICH WATERS WALK

1. From the car park walk across the head of Nantwich Lake and bend left on the surfaced path between the lake and the River Weaver. The lake results from drainage schemes built to manage the brine springs in the area and which fed the Brine Baths Hotel, which stood where the nearby housing estate now is. At the main road, turn right over the Weaver bridge and walk 120 metres to use a metal bridlegate into pasture on the right. Aim right of the small clump of trees ahead, crossing a brook here on a flat bridge between bridlegates. Advance over the low shoulder of the pasture to the corner stock-pens ahead-right. Pass diagonally through and use another bridlegate, putting the fence on your left to walk past three old oaks to a flat crossing of the railway line. Take particular care here; then continue ahead past a pond and alongside the hedge to reach a canal overbridge.

2. Use the steps down to the towpath and turn under the bridge. Beyond this bridge the canal (left) widens out for a short while. This is used as a 'winding hole' by boaters who wish to turn their craft around. It's often a very tricky manoeuvre; dawdle a little if you pass here when someone is turning round! It's now a matter of following the towpath for over 1km. It's a tree-lined route with a wealth of waterbirds to look out for – herons, moorhens and kingfishers amongst them. A long line of moored boats well beyond Bridge 91 heralds the approach to Nantwich aqueduct.

3. Leave the towpath here immediately beyond the metal-railed, cast iron aqueduct, dropping down to the main road. Carefully cross to put the modern flats on your right and the school grounds to your left. This is the extension of Welsh Row; simply walk along this into Nantwich centre. The name Welsh Row derives from the fact that Welsh merchants built properties here. At the end you'll reach the town bridge.

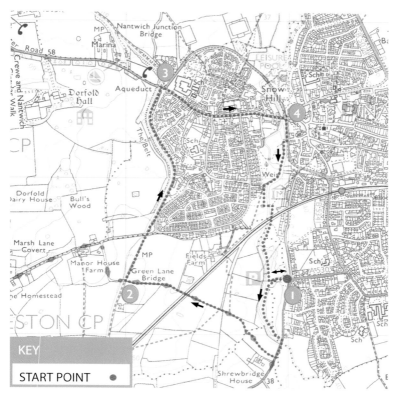

4. To explore the town centre keep ahead. Otherwise turn right alongside the main road. In 150 metres turn right over the brick bridge (accessed from the town centre down Mill Street); then left along the footpath alongside the former cornmill leat. The path soon crosses the old mill weir. Simply keep the River Weaver to your left. Cross the next footbridge and turn right, passing under the railway. Remain beside the river to return to Nantwich Lake and the start point.

GAWSWORTH

An enjoyable ramble linking Shakespeare and marvellous medieval buildings with wildflower-rich canal banks and a dragonfly wonderland

The heart of the old village of Gawsworth is the epitome of all that is English. At one end of a lake is the magnificent medieval church; at the other end the half-timbered facade of a marvellous old manor house draws the eye. Further imposing Georgian houses dapple the immediate area whilst just a short hop away, at one end of the magnificent avenue of lime trees drawing away from the church, is one of England's least spoilt village pubs.

The church of St James the Great dates from the 1400s, built on the site of a much earlier church. The sandstone building stands on a mound above the wooded fringe of one of the village fishponds. In the church are some striking memorials to generations of the Fitton family, one-time residents of the Hall. One family member was Mary Fitton, believed to be the Dark Lady of Shakespeare's sonnets; her unquiet spirit is said to haunt the village.

The Old Hall itself stands back from the pond behind lawns that buffer the building from the outside world. The immediate grounds include the site of a tilting ground, where medieval knightly pursuits were practised. A mile-long wall borders the principal gardens and grounds of the house, which was built in 1480 and remains a private residence. The half-timbered marvel is open to visitors throughout the summer and is renowned for its outdoor theatre presentations.

The walk progresses along the fringe of the grounds before skirting more of the string of fishponds here. Beyond old estate buildings the lane declines to a field path, with lovely views across to the wooded hills of the edge of the Peak District. Crossing the main West Coast Railway, the route strikes across pastures to meet a slightly older line of communication, the Macclesfield Canal.

This cunningly engineered waterway skirls around hillsides and across aqueducts and embankments, meaning only one flight of locks (south of this walk) was needed. In spring and early summer the towpath banks are colourful with a riot of wildflowers. The walk leaves the canal near Moss Head, picking up the line of a long-gone industrial tramroad. This was built to move peat from diggings to the canal for loading onto working boats. Records from the earliest times of the Macclesfield area note that Burgesses of the town had the right to dig peat here at Danes Moss. The horse-drawn, 3 foot-gauge tramroad was in use until the early 1960s. The rare area of lowland raised bog is now a nature reserve renowned for dragonflies and reptiles.

Reaching the village edge, a diversion finds a woodland grave in Maggoty's Wood; a memorial to England's last professional jester!

THE BASICS

Distance: 4¼ miles / 6.8km

Gradient: Largely level

Severity: Easy

Approx. time to walk: 2½ hours

Stiles: Eight, plus handgates and footbridge steps

Map: OS Explorer 268 (Wilmslow, Macclesfield and Congleton)

Path description: Towpath, field paths, tarred lanes; muddy in winter

Start point: Gawsworth (GR SJ 888697)

Parking: Church Lane, Gawsworth, south of the church (SK11 9RJ)

Dog friendly: On leads where appropriate

Public toilets: None

Nearest refreshment: Harrington Arms, Church Lane, Gawsworth

GAWSWORTH WALK

1. From the roadside parking beneath the avenue of beech and lime on Church Lane, head for the churchyard; then put the pond to your right and walk to the nearby T-junction at the top of the water. Views across to the half-timbered Old Hall are idyllic. Turn right on the lane between the ponds; then bend left at the entrance to Gawsworth Old Hall. Pass the old estate buildings, noting the New Hall across the fishpond. As the tarred lane bends right, keep ahead on the rougher track, through a gate and ahead along the path, with the hedge to your right. With some fine views ahead to Macclesfield Forest and the mast-capped Sutton Common, use several more handgates to arrive at a tarred lane. Bear right along this, cross the railway bridge and pass Fodens Farm (left).

2. Just before the lane bends right in a further 100 metres, take the waymarked farm drive to the left. Upon reaching the yard, turn right in front of the barn; then left through a field gate. Use the handgate, left, just past the small open barn and head down-field towards the distant  cottage. Cross a culvert and look ahead for the little footbridge, then rise to the towpath. Turn left alongside the Macclesfield Canal and walk it for 1km to reach swing-bridge 47.

3. Turn left on the track here, shortly crossing a footbridge over the railway. Now pick up the old tree-lined track across Danes Moss. This was the line of the old

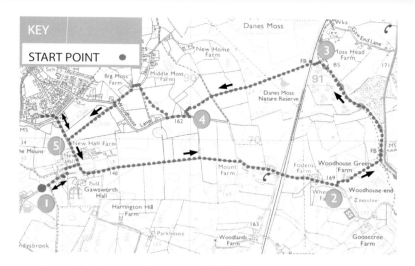

tramroad; sleepers and some track remain. In 800 metres cross straight over the sunken track via a stile and continue along the field edge. Turn hard-left beside the cottage fencing to reach a lane.

4. Turn right; in 150 metres use the kissing gate (right) just past the stable and head for the far-left field corner. Use the stile and advance to the nearby lane. Turn left to the junction; here use the stile opposite into the field. Swap sides at the nearby stile then walk ahead beside the fence (left) to reach Church Lane beneath pine trees.

5. Divert right to the cross-lane. In the woods ahead-left is the jester Maggoty Johnson's grave. Now retrace your steps back along Church Lane, following it to the village ponds, Old Hall and church. To visit the Harrington Arms pub, walk to the far end of the avenue of limes. This very unspoilt farmhouse pub is well worth the detour.

KENT GREEN

A MAGNIFICENT MAGPIE MANSION AND TRANQUIL TOWPATH
AT THE RURAL HEART OF SOUTH CHESHIRE

The Macclesfield Canal slides towards its junction with the older, wider Trent and Mersey Canal just to the north of Kidsgrove. The area lies below the snout of East Cheshire's lofty gritstone ridge, capped by the eye-catching folly castle of Mow Cop. It's a stiff climb up to this ridge; so this walk instead explores the pasturelands lapping the foot of the hill. Along the way are encountered memorable mansions; a peaceful stretch of the canal where industry employed hundreds at the height of the Industrial Revolution; tranquil paths and an old mill. This is lowland Cheshire at its very best.

Across the road from the starting lay-by is one of the National Trust's most visited and loved properties. Little Moreton Hall is a half-timbered gem; surrounded by a deep moat, its twisted structure seems, here and there, to defy the laws of gravity. Commenced before Henry VIII came to the throne, it was completed over a century later after Queen Elizabeth I's death in 1603. The astonishing interior and compact formal gardens repay an extended visit.

The walk passes close to this marvel prior to a path across pastures which reaches the Macclesfield Canal's towpath skirting the foot of the steep slopes rising to Mow Cop. The folly castle on the ridge-top was built in 1754 for Randle Wilbraham, a member of a wealthy family who lived in Rode Hall, close to the route of this walk. It was a summerhouse, designed to 'improve' the prospect from his gardens at Rode Hall, and where he could entertain his guests who were aficionados of the fashionable 'Picturesque' movement that was then all the rage. The folly was donated to the National Trust in 1937.

The canal towpath passes opposite the sturdy Ramsdell Hall and approaches the hamlet of Kent Green. Busy now with narrowboats, the area was originally a wharf where stone and coal taken from workings on Mow Cop was transferred to canal boats from tramroads plummeting down hilly inclines and through long-lost tunnels. The stone was renowned for its qualities for building and for millstones, which were exported widely via the canal network from this corner of Cheshire.

A short stretch along modern suburban roads is followed before the route regains tranquillity on streamside paths and lanes on the old Rode Hall estate. The Hall is renowned for its snowdrops and bluebells, both of which attract many visitors in season; the Georgian Hall itself is open occasionally between April and September. The walk skims the edge of the grounds and passes the old estate mill before field paths and tracks lead back to Little Moreton Hall.

THE BASICS

Distance: 4 miles / 6.4km

Gradient: Virtually level throughout

Severity: Easy

Approx. time to walk: 2¼ hours

Stiles: Ten, plus some kissing gates

Map: OS Explorer 268 (Wilmslow, Macclesfield and Congleton)

Path description: Field paths, towpath, tarred lanes. Two main road crossings

Start point: Little Moreton Hall (GR SJ 831589)

Parking: Large lay-by beside A34 immediately north of the Hall (CW12 4SD)

Dog friendly: On leads where appropriate

Public toilets: None

Nearest refreshment: Rising Sun pub at Kent Green

1. Take the driveway to Little Moreton Hall. Pass by the entrance booth (left) and advance towards the farm. Look for the kissing gate off the bend into the farmyard; here join the well-marked field path. Keep left along the field edge to two more handgates, then ahead-right to a far corner stile. Now it's ahead again up the left edge of several pastures, presently joining a dirt field road to a canal bridge.

2. Immediately before this bridge slip right down the link path onto the towpath and put the Macclesfield Canal to your left. Pass by Ramsdell Hall, then the large marina before reaching the houses of Kent Green (the Rising Sun pub is 100 metres along the road at bridge 87). Remain on the towpath to a point just before the next bridge (No. 89).

3. Slip off the towpath and walk along the lane past the bridge; then through the 'No Entry' sign and ahead to reach the junction with Margery Avenue in another 100 metres. Turn right along this to the left bend in 200 metres. Slip right up the enclosed tarred path; then continue down the close to reach the furthest main road. Carefully cross into the byway named Claphatches and follow this to the cottage at the end of the tarmac. Keep ahead on the grassy path and over a footbridge. In another 30 paces climb the stile on the right into a long meadow. Walk to the line of trees at the far end; at the far side of these join the dirt field road above a brook to reach a lane beside a bridge.

4. Turn left to find Odd Rode Parish Church. Turn right along the main road pavement and walk this for about 400 metres. The grounds of Rode Hall are secluded behind the woods to your left. When you reach the right turn for Rode Mill House (marked with a ruinous millstone) turn along it, passing the evocative, disused old mill

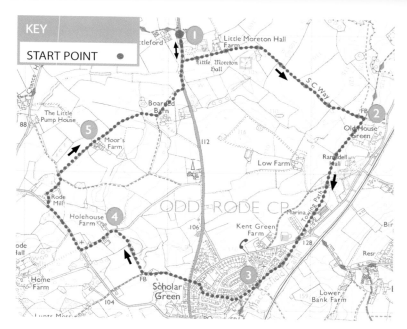

buildings here. The farm lane passes through a band of trees before a long straight reaches Moor's Farm.

5. Look for the well-waymarked path passing left of the complex, joining a hedgerow on your right. Where this bends right beyond a double stile, head half-right towards the copse of trees. Here, bear right on the field track towards Boarded Barn house. Look for the continuing, waymarked field path just before reaching the buildings; head half-left to pass through the line of oaks. At the far side of the field look for the waymarked stile into a hedged path. Two more stiles lead through to the A34. Turn left to the start some 400 metres away.

NORTHWICH WOODLANDS AND BUDWORTH MERE

A GREAT WALK FOR NATURE LOVERS TAKING IN WATERSIDE WOODS AND A REMARKABLE SITE OF TRANSPORT HERITAGE

There's an unexpected industrial heartland to Cheshire centred on the old town of Northwich. It's in the very name of the town — 'wich' denotes a working for salt, and is found in other Cheshire towns like Nantwich, Middlewich and Leftwich. England's biggest salt mine isn't too far away, whilst chemical works still stand beside the River Weaver here.

If this all sounds a little unlikely to offer some enjoyable walking, then think again! Much reclamation has taken place in recent years, creating wildflower meadows, ponds and watery slacks rich with dragon and damselflies, whilst remnants of a vast old country estate offer superb woodland and waterside rambling, lavish with spring ramsons, anemones and bluebells. The area's industrial heritage, too, is fascinating to explore, culminating in an extraordinary engineering marvel which links river and canal at the edge of a vibrant country park. This is a woodland walk *par excellence*!

The walk starts from Marbury Country Park. Curious terraces and levels, avenues of trees and remnants of formal gardens recall the existence of a huge mansion here. Built for the wealthy industrial family, the Smith-Barrys in the 1850s, the immense house saw use as a prisoner-of-war camp in the Second World War before becoming part of the large landholdings of the ICI company. It was demolished in the 1960s. Its location made the most of views across the adjoining Budworth Mere.

The way skims alongside the wood-fringed mere, formed after the last ice age 15,000 years ago, before tracing a stream up a tranquil wooded valley to find the Trent and Mersey Canal towpath. A short stretch is followed before the route starts an exploration of the Northwich Woodlands. Much reclamation of former chemical works land, tree planting and the careful management of ponds and meadows mean that the area is now excellent for wild birds, butterflies and countless other insects.

We follow the bank of the River Weaver to enter Anderton Nature Park. The river is used by a very occasional coaster that has made its way from Runcorn; much more so by leisure craft. As heavy industry appears on the opposite bank, the walk encounters the astonishing Anderton Boat Lift, known in heritage circles as the 'Cathedral of the Waterways'. This spidery structure is reminiscent of a large construction kit. Its purpose is to move narrowboats vertically between the lower River Weaver and the higher Trent and Mersey Canal. This it does by enclosing boats in huge metal baths, or caissons, and raising (or lowering) them 15 meters. The structure dates from the 1850s, and was reopened after being saved from dereliction in 2002. You can take a trip on the lift and nearby waterways from the visitor centre here.

THE BASICS

Distance: 3½ miles / 5.6km

Gradient: Gently undulating

Severity: Easy

Approx. time to walk: 2 hours

Stiles: None, several flights of steps

Map: OS Explorer 267 (Northwich and Delamere Forest)

Path description: Woodland tracks and paths, tarred lanes, towpath

Start point: Marbury Country Park (GR SJ 653764)

Parking: Marbury Country Park car park (pay & display) (CW9 6AT)

Dog friendly: On leads where appropriate

Public toilets: At start and at Boat Lift Centre

Nearest refreshment: Anderton Lift Visitor Centre; pub nearby too

1. From the main car park follow signs to The Mere. There's a bird hide here; it's one of the top 'birding' spots in Cheshire, counting passing ospreys and resident bitterns and water rails amongst many notable species. Put Budworth Mere on your left and follow the waterside path. The imposing church above the far bank is that at Great Budworth. At one point the path jinks inland to avoid a gully, then rejoins the mereside beyond the ice-house and pond. At the little ornate footbridge don't cross it; rather take the path running directly beside Forge Brook, a lovely woodland stroll.

On reaching a fence, turn right to the higher, wider path and left on this. You'll presently reach the canal; here cross the footbridge, double-back beneath it to put the canal on your right and walk to the next overbridge (No. 196).

2. Leave the canal up steps and turn left. Pass the gateway/barrier to reach the nearby signposted junction. Go right a few paces, then left along a wide track beside immature woods. Go through the next gate, then up the ramp to reach Haydn's Pool and a bird hide. Walk round the pool, water on your right. Near a second hide in 400 metres drop left down steps then go right on the wider track alongside Witton Brook. Here you're at the fringe of the Anderton Nature Park, well known for its wildflower meadows.

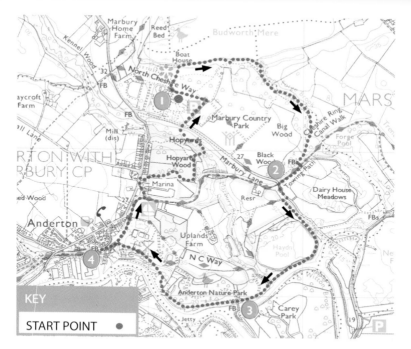

3. At the point where this meets with the River Weaver, ignore the footbridge and continue ahead with the Weaver down to your left. The path slips round a bend, where the partly closed Winnington soda ash works dominates the far bank; note the half-submerged wreck here. Where the path meets a

wider track, chose a way ahead-right to rise to the car park at the Boat Lift. Work your way to the nearby towpath and turn left to visit the remarkable structure.

4. Return along the towpath, canal on your left. At the second overbridge (No. 198), leave the canal, cross the bridge and walk to the main road. Turn right to find, in 70 metres, a barriered path into the rough meadowland and new woodland called Hopyards. Turn along this and wind round to a junction by a bench in 500 metres, where a path departs right, down to cross a footbridge over Marbury Brook. Once across turn left on the streamside path through mature woodland, rich with spring wildflowers, which presently curves right, then left to steps up to Marbury Lane. Cross directly into Marbury Country Park; at the main cross-track turn left to the car park.

LOWER PEOVER WALK

Follow in the footsteps of American generals on a walk between medieval church and Elizabethan mansion

Tranquil, tucked-away villages and eye-catching country houses populate a swathe of north Cheshire. This walk links two of these features, along the way homing in on some Second War history that was partly made here. It starts (and ends) next to a secluded pub that has served the dispersed village of Lower Peover for not far short of 200 years. The Bells of Peover may be named after the peal of bells at the adjacent church, or maybe after a Victorian-era landlord who owned this pub and several others locally and brewed beer for them all. He is apparently loath to leave and haunts the cellar!

It's a smart dining pub today (with a welcome for walkers); but hark back just over 70 years and the old village local it was played host to the leading American generals of the European campaign of World War II, George Patton and Dwight D. Eisenhower. They met in great secrecy in this unlikely spot to discuss and plan the details of Operation Overlord – better known as the D-Day landings and the Allied campaign of June 1944. You'll note that the Stars and Stripes flies next to the Union Jack here in celebration of these meetings.

Right next to the wisteria-covered pub is the lovely half-timbered St Oswald's Church, dating from 1269. Within are memorable rafters, eaves, box-pews and canopied

pews, and a huge parish chest, hewn from a single piece of oak over 700 years ago. Our walk starts from this classic gaggle of village buildings and passes the old village mill before striking across pond-dappled countryside to reach the estate surrounding Peover Hall.

Set well away from any roads, the hall stands in over 500 acres of classic landscaped parkland, designed by the renowned Georgian landscape gardener William Emes in the 1760s. At its core is an Elizabethan mansion built in 1585; additions over the subsequent centuries have produced the remarkable Cheshire-brick building seen today. Equally notable is the large display of topiary which dapples the immediate gardens and lawns. Various themed gardens make Peover one of England's classic country gardens to visit. This walk uses public footpaths through the heart of the estate and gardens. The hall and gardens are open to visitors on Tuesday and Thursday afternoons in summer.

Like the pub, the house too saw war service. It was here that General Patton was based whilst inspecting the training of American Thirrd Army troops for D-Day here deep in the Cheshire countryside. Strangely, it also saw use as a prisoner-of-war camp. It was partially gutted by fire during this period; renovations have been ongoing virtually ever since.

THE BASICS

Distance: 5¼ miles / 8.4km

Gradient: Virtually level throughout

Severity: Easy

Approx. time to walk: 2½ hours

Stiles: Ten, plus gates

Map: OS Explorer 268 (Wilmslow, Macclesfield and Congleton)

Path description: Field paths and roads, tarred lanes. Two main road crossings

Start point: Lower Peover church (GR SJ 744742)

Parking: With consideration on 'The Cobbles' lane leading to the church, or by the church lychgate (WA16 9PZ)

Dog friendly: On leads where appropriate; stiles may be problematic

Public toilets: None

Nearest refreshment: Pubs at start and en route

LOWER PEOVER

1. Head for the handgate in the corner of the churchyard furthest from the pub. A good path strikes away from this across the meadow bordering the lively Peover Eye brook. Look for the footbridge in 500 metres, which crosses the weir feeding the reedy mill leat; cross this and follow the path round to and past the millpond. Through a gate, join a cobbled track, rising gently past the old cornmill and ahead to reach a lane. Turn left to a T-junction; here turn right and follow Free Green Lane for 500 metres, passing three access roads to Free Green Farm.

2. About 150 metres after the last of these roads, turn sharply left at the end of the spinney along a waymarked bridleway which soon passes in front of the farmhouse. Use the gate into the concreted farmyard and bear right, passing in front of the converted brick barns to reach a handgate into a hedged green track. This soon becomes a firm, sandy track which progresses, via a series of gates, between trim hedges, with occasional views across to distant hills to be had. Keep an eye out, too, for the great white dish of the Jodrell Bank radio telescope a few miles away.

3. Beyond Sandylane Farm the main road is reached. Cross carefully and turn right to the bend by the Whipping Stocks pub. Here, join the old driveway to the right of the lodge house and walk this, lined with chestnut trees, across the Peover Estate. Immediately past the short causeway over the end of a pond, fork right along the field road; in another 140 metres use the handgate, right, then accompany the fenceline through more handgates and a copse to a wooded corner with a

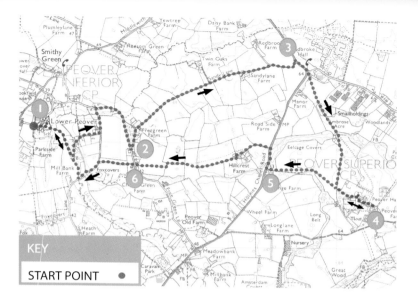

KEY

START POINT ●

final handgate and adjacent stile. Use the waymarked stile and join the firm path winding between the magnificent trees to reach the hard-surfaced driveway curling round to Peover Hall's church, stableyard and view to the house.

4. Turn back and retrace your steps to the wooded corner. Re-cross the stile (but not the handgate); then keep straight ahead beside the fence. At the far end turn left (stile) beside the trees, alongside a horse-gallop. Head for the distant light-painted house; here cut through the fringe of the covert to reach the busy main road.

5. Turn right on the pavement and carefully cross in 200 metres to join the driveway to Hillcrest Farm (hedge on your right). Walk through the gravelled yard of 'Croft Stables' and use the waymarked gate into pasture. Turn right, putting a hedge/fence on your right as you pass an exercise yard. Beyond a corner gate-side stile, keep along the field edge ahead; climb two closely spaced stiles and advance beside the field road to another stile beside a water trough. At the next corner, dog-leg left for 40 metres to find a stile (right) into a final pasture. Head for the left-end of the cottages ahead to find two stiles into a road.

6. Cross into Mill Lane and walk this to the T-junction. Go left to the bridge over the Peover Eye brook in 200 metres. Just beyond this take the path, right, which follows the brook downstream to return to St Oswald's.

WALTON AND THE BRIDGEWATER CANAL

Past a haunted hall to low hills and woods where a renowned fantasy writer once played

This area of north Cheshire is well off the radar of walkers. Just outside Warrington and close to both the M56 motorway and the industrial belt along the Manchester Ship Canal, the countryside is unjustifiably ignored in favour of more rural corners of the county. Prise open the lid, however, and a web of paths, lanes and towpaths is revealed, laid out below low sandstone hills offering some excellent views and surprising tranquillity.

The walk we take is at the heart of the Mersey Forest. This is one of the dozen Community Forests in England, first designated in the early 1990s. The long-term project is to 'green' particular areas of the country by large-scale tree-planting projects, coupled with better management and conservation of existing woodlands. Such environmental improvement is intended to benefit local communities, wildlife and the economy. The Mersey Forest area covers 500 square

miles of north Cheshire and Merseyside. Since 1991 over nine million trees have been planted. It's not a vast, New Forest-like woodland that is emerging; rather a network of wildlife corridors, pocket woods, waterside plantations, nature reserves and environmental projects.

Walton Hall, Park, mini-zoo and gardens is one of Warrington's green lungs. The Hall itself was the home of the renowned local brewery dynasty the Greenall family. Built in the 1830s, it was much larger than the surviving buildings, which are just the east wing and clock tower of this Gothic-style gem. The Greenall family remained in residence until 1941; by 1945 much of the old estate had become a publically owned park and gardens. The hall is said to be haunted by the ghost of Lady Daresbury, a member of the Greenall family!

The walk slips out of the parkland and rises gently up Hill Cliffe. Great views develop as the route skirts woodland before passing Appleton Reservoir, a good spot for a bit of birdwatching. Small woods and back lanes now take the walk towards the Bridgewater Canal. One child who played in these undulating pastures and spinneys would have been Charles Lutwidge Dodgson, better known as the writer of *Alice in Wonderland*, Lewis Carroll. He spent his childhood at nearby Daresbury vicarage, where his father was the curate.

Descending a quiet, walled lane, the walk reaches the Bridgewater Canal. This is the first major canal of the early Industrial Revolution. Part of a system built for Francis Egerton, 3rd Duke of Bridgewater and owner of coalmines at Worsley, near Manchester, it connected Manchester and the Mersey Estuary at Runcorn. It opened in stages from 1761, with the renowned engineer James Brindley in charge of the project. From the village of Moore the towpath is followed through pastures and cornfields back to Walton.

THE BASICS

Distance: 5 miles / 8km

Gradient: Several gradual ascents and descents

Severity: Easy

Approx. time to walk: 2½ hours

Stiles: Four, plus handgates

Map: OS Explorer 276 (Bolton, Wigan and Warrington)

Path description: Lanes, woodland paths, parkland, towpath; one main-road crossing

Start point: Walton Hall (GR SJ 601853)

Parking: Pay & display car park, Walton Hall (WA44 6SN)

Dog friendly: On leads where appropriate

Public toilets: At start

Nearest refreshment: Café at start, pub near end

1. From the main car park cross one of the bridges into the park and turn right with the road. Bend left and rise up to the Hall. Bend left in front of it, then find the nearby bandstand. Walk up the wide, sloping lawn with the putting greens on your left. Bend left near the top of the lawn to join the rail-lined, tree-shaded path between  golf courses, presently reaching Hough's Lane. Turn left on it for around 150 metres, then go right along the driveway signed as a bridlepath to Hillcliffe. As you reach Hillfoot Farm, turn right up the fenced path and rise gently to a fenced cross-path. Turn right on this, which soon enters a woodland fringe and advances just above a series of golf fairways, eventually reaching the narrow Firs Lane.

2. Turn right down this and remain with it past houses, bending right at Daintith Farm. In a further 150 metres you'll reach the near-end of the dam holding back Appleton Reservoir. Climb the few steps and take the path to the left, which curls round a tongue of land before rejoining a tarred lane. Turn right 40 paces, then right again onto another waterside path. This soon reaches a wooded corner beyond a short causeway. Go ahead on the waymarked path over the footbridge and turn left through the trees (leaving the reservoir). At the streamside corner turn right on the wide path to the woodland edge. Turn left over the stiled footbridge and walk to the next corner. Turn right and trace the hedgeline (left) over a stile and through to a lane.

3. Turn left; traffic is light but fast, so be aware. Pass Hatton Lodge Cottages; then in another 230 metres take the signposted handgate on the right. Cross the nearby culvert, then turn right to a handgate 15 metres above the next corner. Keep ahead along the long left field boundary. At the corner cut through the neck of woodland via handgates. Turn right along its far edge around two field edges outside the old oakwoods. When the woods turn away right, use the handgate and keep straight across the field, heading for the slim phone mast to reach the main road.

4. Cross carefully to the right and join Hobb Lane. Walk this usually tranquil back road all the way to its far end beyond a canal bridge. Turn left; slip onto the towpath and double back to pass beneath the bridge. Remain with the Bridgewater Canal for over 2km to return to Walton Lea bridge at the entrance to Walton Hall park. Climb the sturdy metal steps to find the car park.

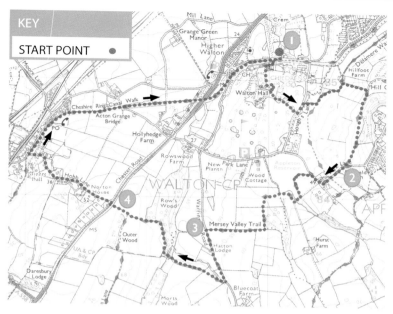

AUDLEM AND THE SHROPPIE

OBSERVE THE UPS AND DOWNS OF A CHALLENGING CANAL STAIRCASE HIDDEN IN THE CHESHIRE COUNTRYSIDE

The pretty little town of Audlem nestles in southern Cheshire, close to the Shropshire border in the higher reaches of the valley of the River Weaver. It's one of the oldest market towns in the county, awarded a charter to hold regular markets in AD 1295, although nowadays the nearby town of Nantwich is where the stallholders and traders congregate.

The substantial parish church of St James recalls these more prosperous days. It has stood on a mound high above the marketplace for nearly 750 years. Beside its churchyard wall stands the covered buttermarket; a miniature marvel supported

on sturdy stone pillars. In days of yore people congregated here not only to trade and barter but also to be entertained. Beside the churchyard steps is a large granite boulder known as the bear-baiting stone. To this were attached, by nose-ring and chain, hapless creatures who would be 'encouraged' to perform by their travelling owners.

The town is dappled by old buildings and well repays a leisurely stroll along its back lanes and ginnels. Today's main attractions, however, lie just to the west of the centre. At the foot of a gentle hill stands one of the old town mills (others dot the countryside around), commanding a position next to the Shropshire Union Canal – 'The Shroppie'. This and the nearby inns show how the town quickly took advantage of the opportunities offered by the new transport highway. Opened in 1835 as the Liverpool and Birmingham Junction Canal, it was engineered to the plans of the renowned Thomas Telford and formed one link in a chain of waterways linking Birmingham and the Black Country to the Mersey Estuary. Flour was just one of the products exported by Audlem farmers; another frequent cargo was Cheshire Cheese. An old crane and wharves recall busier days here.

This walk takes advantage of the canal's towpath as it rises from the valley of the Weaver up a flight of 15 locks to gain the higher level of the Shropshire plateau here; a rise of just 93 feet but a supreme effort for boaters. In the canal's heyday a service of flyboats linked Audlem to the cities of Chester and Birmingham; high-speed (relatively!) services taking goods and passengers on overnight journeys. Today's scene is less manic, with a continual stream of leisure narrowboats challenging the flight of locks. In season a day-boat offers trips to and from a large marina just north of the town.

The walk leaves the canalside a little before the top of the flight, meandering down into the valley of the little River Duckow. A pretty stretch of alder and willow-lined meadows returns to Audlem for a final circuit of the wharf.

THE BASICS

Distance: 4 miles / 6.4km

Gradient: Several gentle ascents and descents

Severity: Easy

Approx. time to walk: 2½ hours

Stiles: Eleven, plus several kissing gates and a few steps

Map: OS Explorer 257 (Crewe and Nantwich)

Path description: Towpath, field paths, tarred lanes

Start point: Audlem (GR SJ 659436)

Parking: Village car park, Cheshire Street (free) (CW3 0AH)

Dog friendly: On leads where appropriate. May need to be carried at lock gate

Public toilets: In Audlem

Nearest refreshment: Pubs and cafés in Audlem

AUDLEM AND THE SHROPPIE WALK

1. Turn right from the car park entrance and walk to The Square. On your left is the quaint old buttermarket and bear stone. Cross into Vicarage Lane and descend this round the bend. Bear right across the little town green to cross the footbridge over the brook. Turn immediately right and keep the brook on your right. In 375 metres angle left away from the brook, up the grassy pasture and past two redundant stiles to steps and a stile onto the canal towpath. Turn left and head up beside the flight of locks.

2. At bridge 76 (Lock 3) swap sides of the canal and use the stile onto a path along the other bank. At a stile in 300 metres turn right along the hedged path. This becomes a lane past cottages at Coxbank; at the junction keep right to reach the old Primitive Methodist chapel. Bear left here on Chapel Lane to reach the main road.

3. Cross carefully into Heywood Lane and walk this high-hedged road to cross the bridge over the River Duckow. In another 20 metres take the stile (right) onto a field path, keeping to the break of slope parallel to but well above the river. Pass under electricity wires; in another 150 metres are a stile and handgate. Go ahead 50 metres then drop right to a footbridge beside a gnarled willow. Once across (muddy here!) turn left and aim for the three tall alders in the hedge at the lower far side of the pasture, beneath which is a plank bridge (below more electricity wires). Head now for the wood-shingle stable block, crossing stiles to reach a gate into a lane just below it.

4. Bear left and pass Swanbach Mill to reach the A525. Turn right, uphill to reach Heywood's Ridge on your right. In another 25 metres take the path right, up the steps and along the enclosed path. Emerging beside a house, use the kissing gate opposite into a fenced field-edge path. At the corner walk down the tarred driveway to the A529. Look right for the footbridge in trees on the other side of the road and trace the path left off it beside the brook. In 50 metres, just past a manhole cover, bear right away from the brook to walk up the sloping pasture and past the stand of tall trees to find a stile at a lock. Carefully cross the lock-gate to the towpath and turn left to Audlem.

5. Remain beside the canal past the wharf. Immediately before Lock 15 (numbers on the lock gates) turn back-right up a waymarked (on a telegraph pole) path up to a handgate; then follow the distinct path across two pastures to the kissing gate beyond a horse exercise yard. Turn right on the tarred drive; then in 10 metres go left along the sunken path to reach the main road. Cross this, go right and pass 'Broadways' road. In another 20 metres slip left on the enclosed path which soon widens to a tarred track called Churchfields. Turn right at the bottom to reach the buttermarket. Turn right back to the car park.

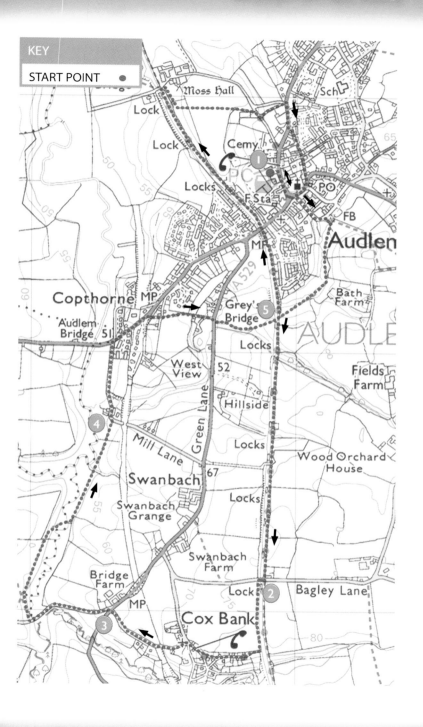

KEY

START POINT ●

Moss Hall

Lock

Lock

Lock

Sch

Cemy.

Locks

F. Sta.

PO

FB

MP

Audlen

Copthorne MP

Grey's Bridge

Bath Farm

AUDLE

Audlem Bridge 51

Locks

West View 52

Fields Farm

Green Lane

Hillside

Locks

Mill Lane

Swanbach 67

Wood Orchard House

Swanbach Grange

Locks

Bridge Farm

Swanbach Farm

MP

Lock

Bagley Lane

Cox Bank

STYAL AND THE BOLLIN VALLEY

EXPLORE AN ALLURING INDUSTRIAL HAMLET AND FABULOUS
WOODED GORGE IN THE SHADOW OF MANCHESTER AIRPORT

The River Bollin starts its vigorous course high up in the hilly country of the Macclesfield Forest, close to Cheshire's highest land in the Peak District. As it slides through lively sections and languid stretches of pasture it has been exploited for many centuries, with corn mills being recorded in the famous Domesday Book survey of AD1086. It was during the Industrial Revolution in the 18th century, however, that the river came into its own, with its waters used for bleaching, dyeing and power generation.

By far the most significant site was tucked away in a particularly secluded and tortuous section of the valley at Styal. In 1783 the eyes of businessman Samuel Greg alighted on this bucolic corner of the realm. His family were already established mill-owners in the rapidly expanding centre of Manchester. Greg realised that a 'greenfield' site would allow him to exploit the new technology that was being developed to boost production and profit. Within a year the steep sides of

the Bollin were echoing to the sounds of machinery in the state-of-the-art Quarry Bank Mill, driven by the considerable power of the river's water harnessed by a waterwheel.

The business boomed; Greg found it necessary to extend the works, source new employees and develop the use of technology further. Today's chocolate-box village of thatched cottages and prim terraces was purpose-built as a planned industrial settlement. For its day it was top-notch, with generous room supplied in the cottages; basic facilities unseen in urban housing and social and educational provision that was a shining example in its day. He also built the Apprentice House, where child labourers were housed and fed; many of these were street-children, or 'imported' from places as far away as London.

The village is at the start of the walk. The way then meanders along old lanes before bumping into Ringway, these days known as Manchester Airport. The old airfield, founded in 1937, was an important practice ground for parachute training during the Second World War. Huge expansion in the past 20 years has seen it become one of Britain's busiest airports. It's a fascinating, if occasionally noisy, ramble beside the newest runway before the route drops into the valley of the River Bollin.

The contrast is striking. The sound of aeroplane engines is largely muffled by the steep sides of the heavily wooded valley. The path strings upstream past specimen trees planted for the Greg family, presently reaching an enchanting area of tight river loops, footbridges, surprise views and wildflower-rich old woodland. Countless paths explore these National Trust-owned woods; an ideal place to linger before reaching the village again and paths beside pastures to the absorbing mill, one of the country's finest 'living' museums.

THE BASICS

Distance: 3 miles / 4.8km

Gradient: Several gradual ascents and descents; many steps

Severity: Moderate

Approx. time to walk: 2 hours

Stiles: Lots of handgates and steps

Map: OS Explorer 268 (Wilmslow, Macclesfield and Congleton)

Path description: Lanes, sandy bridle paths, woodland paths

Start point: Styal (GR SJ 837845)

Parking: Roadside beyond The Ship Inn, Altrincham Road (SK9 4JE)

Dog friendly: On leads where appropriate

Public toilets: None

Nearest refreshment: Tearoom and pub in Styal; café at Mill

1. With the pub, or cricket ground, on your right, walk along Altrincham Road away from the village centre. It's usually a quiet back road. Remain with it for nearly 1km, passing by Holly Lane on your right to reach a junction with Moss Lane. At this split, fork left, signposted for Oversley Ford, and advance along the gated old road used by occasional farm traffic. Just before it reaches a security gate in the fencing surrounding Manchester Airport, turn left by trees up the waymarked cycleway to the crest of the bank and turn right along this. Plane-spotters will delight in the views across the airport's two runways. The path soon joins a wider way outside the perimeter fence. Remain with this for another 400 metres or so to reach a 'Private, Authorised Access Only' sign. Here branch left on a gated path that drops away from the runways and around a sharp zigzag.

2. Immediately after these bends turn left to and through a handgate into the woods. This is an undulating route within the screen of trees lining the Bollin's banks. It soon becomes more wooded, threading a way above the river past a string of magnificent specimen trees. Emerging from the woods for a short while, look out for Highland cattle grazing the sloping pastures. Re-entering the woods the way becomes more challenging, with flights of steps rising well above the river before plunging back down again.

The walk crosses the sturdy Giants Castle Bridge and threads a braided way through the woods, presently rising up and down more flights of steps before regaining the riverside path at Oxbow Bridge.

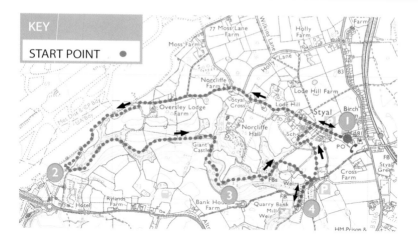

3. Cross this bridge and turn left. In 125 metres turn right at the fork along the level path beside the Bollin. Once over the smaller Kingfisher Bridge the path drifts left and uphill, steps gaining height above the wooded dingle on your left. Just before another ornate bridge on your left, turn right along a fenced path out of the woods. Cross directly over the dirt track and keep ahead to reach a tarred drive. Turn downhill to visit Quarry Bank Mill.

4. Return then uphill to the path, left, for Styal Village, a fenced way past the Apprentice House garden. This strikes through to the old cross. Spend time now exploring the old village centre where the millworkers once lived. Work through to Altrincham Road and go right to find The Ship Inn.

ALDERLEY EDGE

WALK THROUGH A WIZARD'S DOMAIN PAST FABULOUS
VIEWPOINTS AND THROUGH WONDERFUL WOODLANDS

The town of Alderley Edge grew with the railway. A scattered farming hamlet developed as a country retreat for well-to-do industrialists and professionals whose fortunes came from the commercial hub of Manchester. Rising steeply from the flat-lands of the Cheshire Plain, the thickly wooded sandstone edge became dappled with mansions and villas, climbing to the lip of the escarpment and the undulating countryside beyond.

But these wealthy residents were far from the first to take advantage of the location. The earliest evidence is to be found in the unexpected landscape hidden amidst the marvellous woodlands now cared for by the National Trust. Scattered liberally across these acres are reminders of a copper-mining industry that started well before the Romans reached Britain. Bronze Age people mined here 4,000 years ago; a wooden spade found by Victorian miners in the 1870s has been dated to about 1750 BC. In 1995 a hoard of Roman coins was discovered secreted in a shaft; they too are thought to have mined here.

Georgian and Victorian miners continued to explore for copper and other minerals such as lead and even silver. The various workings passed on the walk result from such expansion. By late Victorian times work had all but ceased, leaving scars on the top of the Edge and adjoining heathland which still tantalise today. Occasional open days by Derbyshire Caving Club allow curious visitors to explore the more accessible workings.

It's unlikely that such visitors will encounter the Edge's most famous residents. Folklore tells that a farmer returning from market along the old road across the Edge was accosted by a grey-clad stranger who offered to buy his unsold horse. Keen to profit, the farmer followed the stranger to Stormy Point, at which place the man produced a wand and struck the rock-face, revealing iron gates into an underground chamber. Here were knights of old and white steeds awaiting, the Wizard told the farmer, the call to aid England in her hour of need. The Wizard rewarded the farmer handsomely from a treasure chest and guided him back to the surface. The next moment no sign of the cavern, Wizard or troops could be found. This

legend is a lynchpin in the absorbing children's book *The Weirdstone of Brisingamen* by Alan Garner.

Today, Stormy Point is one of the highlights of the Edge's spider's web of paths and tracks. Stately beech, oak and pine woods part to reveal extraordinary views to the Peak District's hills and the West Pennines beyond Manchester. An Armada Beacon in 1588 took advantage of this lofty position; this too is passed on the walk.

THE BASICS

Distance: 3½ miles / 5.6km

Gradient: Undulating with several climbs

Severity: Easy

Approx. time to walk: 2 hours

Stiles: Two, plus gap-stiles and handgates

Map: OS Explorer 268 (Wilmslow, Macclesfield and Congleton)

Path description: Woodland tracks and paths, tarred lanes, some very steep drops

Start point: The Edge, Alderley Edge (GR SJ 860772)

Parking: National Trust (NT) pay car park on Alderley Edge (SK10 4UB) (also limited free parking at Point 2)

Dog friendly: On Leads where appropriate

Public toilets: National Trust car park

Nearest refreshment: The Wizard pub and tearoom, at start

ALDERLEY EDGE WALK

1. Turn left from the National Trust (NT) car park and walk 100 metres to Bradford Lane. Turn right along this; bend left on Finlow Hill Lane, then left again in 450 metres. Already there are great views across to the shapely hills above Macclesfield. Some 50 metres beyond the stables use a waymarked stile, left, and cut through the woods to a road. Cross into the driveway opposite, then go left along the grass-centred track. Pass by the house, presently reaching the derelict Edge House Farm. Skirt to its left as waymarked; cross a crossing path by a cottage and keep ahead to fencing and a major track junction. Use the left-hand gate and advance half-left on the lesser path into the woods. At the path junction bend left past fenced old quarry workings, continuing then straight ahead over a cross-path to reach the main road beside Beacon Lodge.

2. Cross and join the woodland path past an NT sign. Head slightly left over the open area, joining a braided path to reach a point near a field on your left. Here also is an information board about Hagg Fold cottages. Continue past the nearby NT wooden plinth for about 30 metres; then turn right on a narrower path through the trees and directly away from the field. In 100 metres this passes above a gully (right) where an adit (tunnel) of the old West Mine disappears underground. Drift right to the nearby woodland edge gate just past a pond. Use the gap stile into pasture and head slightly left to pass just left of a shrub-shrouded pond. Aim for the right-end of the brick wall and an enclosed path to Macclesfield Road.

3. Cross into Underwood Road, passing some of the huge houses on this favoured side of the Edge. At the end go right, up Woodbrook Road. Follow it until it descends and bends right. Here, at the distinctive stepped stone wall, go sharp-L

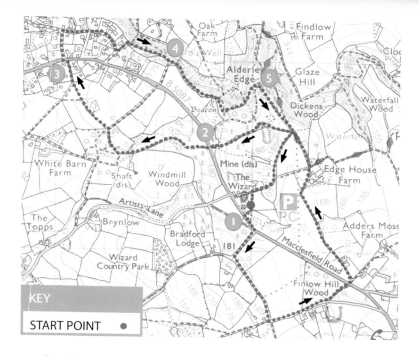

KEY

START POINT ●

through a gap stile into a rising fenced path. This soon enters woods via a gap stile by a rusty gas-standard. Favour the falling path; in 100 metres turn right up the wider path, soon passing the Wizard's Well below a low cliff. Just past this bear right between old gateposts, then turn left to emerge onto Castle Rock, the first fabulous viewpoint here.

4.   Remain on the highest path, with the field on your right. Skirting a wall you'll soon reach steps up to the Armada Beacon, the site of a Bronze Age burial mound. Stand behind the plinth so you can read the plaque. Look directly ahead and drop down different steps, then ahead on a descending wide woodland path. This crosses the head of a dingle and a small flat bridge before rising to reach Stormy Point. There's a remarkable series of crumbled cliffs and old workings to explore – carefully!

5.   Put the view to your left and join the higher, compacted path (not the cliff-edge path) back into the woods beside a fence heading away from Stormy Point (not the path signed car park). Keep ahead-left on the wider path at the fork in 100 metres. At the wooden-rail fence in 300 metres, use a handgate and turn right on the wide woodland-edge track, which meanders past more old mineworkings through to the pub and car park.

PRIMROSEHILL WOOD

WALK IN A QUIETER CORNER OF DELAMERE FOREST TO SECLUDED VALES AND RAVINES

This outlying area of Delamere Forest stands well away from the much more popular heart of the forest. Far more peaceful, the hillside woodland is particularly rich with wildflowers throughout the spring and summer, with great stands of foxgloves a particular feature. A network of woodland paths and tracks make exploring this area of open access land a doddle.

Before the woodland stroll, however, is an undulating walk along this western fringe of the mid-Cheshire ridge, part of the sandstone spine at Cheshire's heart. The walk starts from a parking area high above Kelsall at King's Gate. This probably marks the site of an entrance into the former Royal Forest hunting chase that existed here in Saxon and later times. A brief flirtation with a quiet lane passes a village pond before entering open pasture across Castle Hill.

The castle in question was Kelsborrow Castle; an example of a promontory fort built sometime in the late Bronze Age or early Iron Age nearly 3,000 years ago. Its site on a corner of land jutting out from the escarpment was made easily defensible by building a line of steep ditches and a bank across the neck of land. The bank was topped by a wooded palisade to improve the protection offered. It's one of at least half-a-dozen such forts along the length of the sandstone spine. All that can be seen are the vague shadow of the bank and ditch in the cattle pastures here.

The walk then strikes along a path etched along the side of a deep, steep little valley at Boothsdale. This was long a favoured destination for day-trippers in Victorian and Edwardian times, when the area was, rather ambitiously, named 'Little Switzerland'. There are exquisite views on crystal clear days across Cheshire to the distant range of the Clwydian Hills in north-east Wales. As the path reaches the foot of the wooded scarp, there's chance to divert to a handy nearby pub. Also on the route of the walk is a cider farm above the hamlet of Willington.

A quiet lane rises consistently up another of the area's steep little valleys, advancing along a gentle ridge, with more grand views, to find the entrance to Primrosehill Wood. Just along from here is the chalybeate spring called Whistlebitch Well. This was very popular in the time of Queen Elizabeth I, when health-spa drinking was all the rage; its waters apparently cured blindness, deafness and the ague.

Progressing through the tranquil woods, we'll visit the secluded Urchin's Kitchen ravine. This ferny chasm is thought to be the result of sudden and concentrated erosion by glacial meltwaters escaping under pressure from beneath the great ice-sheet that covered Cheshire 15,000 years ago.

THE BASICS

Distance: 4 miles / 6.4km

Gradient: Several ascents and descents

Severity: Moderate

Approx. time to walk: 2½ hours

Stiles: None, several kissing gates

Map: OS Explorer 267 (Northwich and Delamere Forest)

Path description: Woodland and field paths, tarred lanes

Start point: King's Gate (GR SJ 535678)

Parking: Woodland edge car park at King's Gate (free) (CW6 0PF approx.)

Dog friendly: On leads where appropriate

Public toilets: None

Nearest refreshment: The Boot Inn, Boothsdale

PRIMROSEHILL WOOD WALK

1. With your back to the parking area turn right along the lane. Bend left with it to the grassy area with a tree-shaded pond on your left. You should turn left to pass in front of Lower Fold cottage (*not* beside the pond), looking for the Willington fingerpost indicating a path below holly trees. Beyond, use a kissing gate into a fenced way across pasture and through another gate. To your right are insignificant ridges in the field and a curved band of trees marks the edge of a steep slope. This is all part of the hillfort at Kelsborrow, which at its peak covered around nine acres of this elevated site overlooking the plain below.

At the far corner a kissing gate gives onto a stepped path which strikes along the flank of Boothsdale, trimming the fringe of woodland. It's a beautiful view west which now accompanies as the way descends easily into this secret dale sliced deep into Cheshire's sandstone spine. At cottages it become an access track, then a lane. The way to The Boot Inn is sharp-right along the hedged path near the startling new house. Otherwise remain on the tarred lane.

2. At the junction the way is left up Rough Low. On your right at this point is the cider farm shop. The quiet road climbs steadily across the wooded slope of Pearl Hole dingle before bending right as Tirley Lane and levelling along the modest ridge-top. Remain with this, harvesting

exceptional views across Cheshire and down the wooded sandstone spine, for 1.5km to the junction signed right for Utkinton.

3. Turn left here on the rough lane to a cattery. It's also waymarked as the Delamere Loop bridleway. This is the fringe of Primrosehill Wood. The track snakes through the woodland; the iron-roofed shed to your right at one point covers the Whistlebitch healing well. At the gates to Primrosehill House turn right, remaining on the firm track to the foot of the woods.

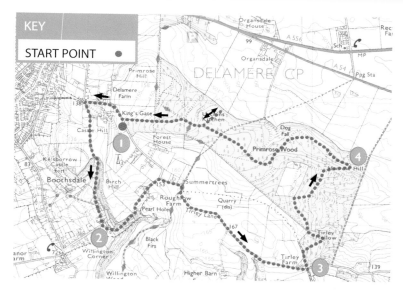

4. Bend sharp-left, staying in the woods on the now gradually rising track, soon skirting newly established woodland. Keep left at a fork, then left again at a junction marked by a memorial bench. Shortly afterwards take the opportunity (signed) to turn right to explore the Urchin's Kitchen miniature gorge, Return then to the main track, turn right and then bend left, rising gently uphill back up to King's Gate.

DELAMERE FOREST

The Earl of Chester, William the Conqueror's cousin Hugh d'Avranches, took over a Saxon hunting estate and greatly extended it as a Royal Forest. Eventually the Forests of Mara and Mondrum covered 60 square miles of Cheshire. Today's Delamere Forest is the remnant section of Mara; 'Delamere' derives from French and refers to the meres that exist in the area. These Royal Forests were hunting reserves where the nobility, clergy and monarch would hunt deer, boar, wolves and even bears.

Access was strictly controlled and the woods were carefully managed for the hunt. Remarkably, although piecemeal clearance took place over the centuries, it was not until 1812 that the stringent Forest Law was lifted and the Mara estate was subjected to enclosure awards. This redistribution of land coincided with the wars against Napoleon; the result was that Delamere was planted with pines, oaks and beech to ensure a long-term resource for building naval vessels for future conflicts. These plantings form the bulk of today's forest, offering contrasting walking. There are few really old trees in Delamere; this walk explores a variety of landscapes including grand stands of broadleaves and pine-sheltered meres. There are few deer here nowadays; instead the area is renowned for birds and insects – the Forest's logo is a dragonfly.

The walk starts at the Linmere Centre. Our ramble cuts past the 'Go Ape' attraction before reaching the vast watery landscape of Blakemere. Until the 1990s this didn't exist as such; the area was marshy, dark pinewoods with very little life. The decision was taken to recreate aspects of the landscape which existed in medieval times, including the mere that may well have given the forest its name. Thus in 1992 the area was cleared of the poor-quality trees and allowed to flood. Today it's a slightly eerie landscape of reeds, dead trees, islets and still, open water that reflects the sky particularly well. It's a major nesting area for very noisy black-headed gulls and alive with countless other species.

The walk skirts around the mere before meandering through old woodland and across the Chester to Manchester railway to find the secluded little Black Lake. This is Dragonfly Central; it's worth spending time at the water's edge to watch these astonishing creatures (and the smaller damselflies) as they hunt from stands of reeds. The walk presently heads out of the woods, where the longer route then climbs steadily to the wonderful viewpoint at Pale Heights. Seven modern-day standing stones represent the seven counties visible from this modest hilltop. The slightly lower hill adjoining to the east is Eddisbury Hill, capped by the site of a hillfort from where, it is said, King Alfred's daughter Aethelflaeda fought the invading Danes 1,100 years ago.

THE BASICS

Distance: 4 miles / 6.4km or 5½ miles / 8.8km

Gradient: Several gradual ascents and descents

Severity: Easy (moderate for longer walk)

Approx. time to walk: 2¼ or 3½ hours

Stiles: None, a few handgates

Map: OS Explorer 267 (Northwich and Delamere Forest)

Path description: Forest tracks and paths, tarred lanes

Start point: Delamere Forest Park, behind Delamere Station (GR SJ 549705)

Parking: Linmere car park (pay & display) (CW8 2JD)

Dog friendly: On leads where appropriate

Public toilets: Linmere visitor area

Nearest refreshment: Cafés at Linmere and at Delamere Station

Public transport: Trains to Delamere Station on Chester to Manchester Piccadilly line (Tel: Traveline 0871 200 2233)

DELAMERE FOREST WALK

1. Find and cross the bridge over the railway towards the 'Go Ape' course. Remain on this firm road past the houses (left) and a barrier, continuing to a left bend in another 150 metres. Here; fork right on a lesser forest track; swing right and walk through to a T-junction close to a 'Go Ape' structure. Turn right

along the wide track that circles the atmospheric Blakemere lake. At any junctions keep left, continuing around the fringe of the lake for about 1.5km. Be very wary at the water's edge, as thick moss disguises marshy areas of water that look solid – but aren't! Ignore any paths or tracks to the right. In time the mere disappears beneath heathery mire. You'll eventually reach a significant junction marked by a picnic table on your right (and a path to the left out towards the mire).

2. Turn right onto the waymarked Delamere Way (and the red bootmark walk) and walk this beneath a strand of graceful beech and oak. A reedy mere soon appears in the dip on your right. In 400 metres you'll reach a main forestry road. Turn right and walk 50 metres to locate, on the left beneath a gnarled, twisted chestnut, the waymarked Delamere Way. Join this well-defined dirt path winding through lovely woodland to reach a T-junction with a wide compacted-surface track in 750 metres. Turn left (leaving Delamere Way); then in another 150 metres fork right on the lesser track, looping round with

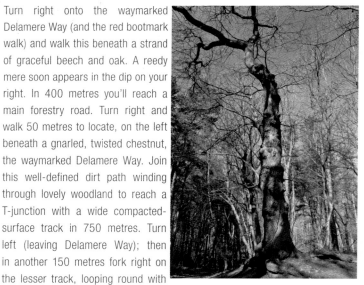

this to reach another track beside a railway bridge. Cross this bridge and turn immediately left on a dirt path which winds, always within 30 metres of the fence guarding the railway cutting (left), beneath a succession of magnificent old chestnuts and pines. You'll reach another railway bridge.

3. Don't cross it. Rather; turn right 20 paces, then fork left on a narrow path through to the edge of the secluded little Black Lake. This is a good spot for dragonflies. Walk past the bench; at the rear end of the lake peel left on the path which soon meets a cross-path. Turn right and walk to the major junction of ways in

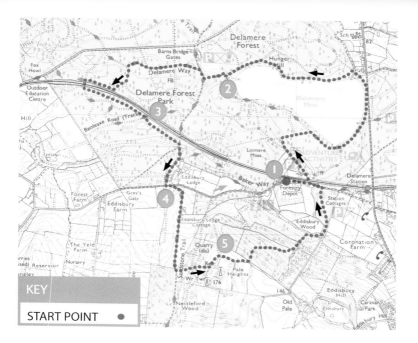

250 metres. Here; bear right along the furthest, widest roadway. In 100 metres fork right (signed Sandstone Trail) on a path up a wooded dingle, then by a pasture to reach a woodside roadway. Turn left to the nearby junction.

4.   For the **shorter walk** simply remain on the roadway to return to Linmere. For the full route turn right along the driveway (Sandstone Trail) that curves right and starts a gentle climb. Past a farmhouse it becomes a fenced track, rising to a woodland corner gate in another 500 metres. Turn left on the path; cross over the more substantial track in 100 meters and rise ahead-left to a wide sandy track near aerials, heading left to the viewpoint on Pale Heights.

5.   Leave on the path between the 'Derbyshire' and 'Staffordshire' standing stones, then in 150 metres fork left on the wide path that drops steadily to and through the immature woodland. At the bottom turn left on the tarred lane. In 100 metres slip ahead-left through the hedge-gap onto a path which drifts through more new woodland to reach the main Linmere access road. Go left (uphill) to the main car park in 250 metres.

BULKELEY HILL AND RAW HEAD

Marvellous views, magical woodland and unexpected heritage amidst rippling sandstone hills

Cheshire's sandstone spine essentially splits the county in two. This string of knobbly hills, knolls and ridges stretches from the Mersey in the north to the edge of the Shropshire meres near Whitchurch. The line of undulating hills, split by gaps of rich farmland, is

well wooded in many places and allows for some lovely walks in countryside rich with wildflowers. To either side of these modest uplands, the Cheshire Plain stretches to horizons marked by the distant, purpley high lands of the Clwydian Range to the west, the Peak District to the east.

A country lane slides from one of the gaps in the ridge as Copper Mine Lane. The name is a giveaway, as in this most unlikely location copper was mined for hundreds of years. It's possible that the Romans worked the ore here, but the scant remains visible today date from Victorian times, when the industry peaked before declining to closure from the 1860s. The brick chimney in the field (passed at the end of the walk) is that of a Cornish beam engine, used to help drain the mines. About six shafts were worked, the deepest one being beside the chimney; Engine Mine at 156 feet deep.

Higher up on the ridge, which is followed in part by the well-signed Sandstone Trail, the route climbs to the snout of Bulkeley Hill. Owned by the National Trust, the hill's highest acres are dappled by some extraordinary old sweet chestnut trees, their twisted boughs and branches spreading wide over the woodland floor. There are some great views through the trees here, off the precipitous edge of the ridge east towards the Peak District's hills and north to Peckforton Point and the Peckforton Hills.

Also here is another unexpected industrial relic. A waterworks at Bulkeley was created in the 1950s to supply water to The Potteries. A steeply inclined tram road allowed equipment and construction goods to be raised to a holding reservoir at the hilltop, from where water flows in pipes by gravity to distant Staffordshire. Views down it are giddying.

The route glides easily through these mixed broadleaf and pine woods before dropping gently to meet a wide sandy track looping south alongside steep pastures. The way then strikes through more undulating woodlands to reach Raw Head. This fabulous viewpoint is the highest point on the Sandstone Trail. On clear days the shapely  Clwydian Hills, the more remote Berwyn Mountains and the uplands of Snowdonia can be seen, as can Chester Cathedral and the two more distant cathedrals in Liverpool. Nearer to hand, just to the south on Bickerton Hill stands one of the line of hillforts that commanded these wooded hills 2,000 years ago.

THE BASICS

Distance: 3¾ miles / 6km

Gradient: Several gradual ascents and descents

Severity: Moderate

Approx. time to walk: 2½ hours

Stiles: Two, plus handgates and several flights of steps

Map: OS Explorer 257 (Crewe and Nantwich)

Path description: Woodland paths, tarred lanes, farm roads; some steep drops path-side

Start point: Gallantry Bank (GR SJ 517543)

Parking: Lay-by on A534 opposite Copper Mine Lane (SY14 8AY)

Dog friendly: On leads where appropriate

Public toilets: None

Nearest refreshment: The Bickerton Poacher pub (half a mile/800m east of starting point)

1. Carefully cross the main road into Copper Mine Lane – the old chimney is clearly seen – and wind gently uphill for 500 metres. The lane breaks free of the trees and levels amidst pastures; in another 350 metres look for the cattle-pen on your right amidst a flourish of gates. A footpath fingerpost points the way alongside a fence towards the trees.

Within the woodland edge keep straight ahead on the rising path beneath pines, a Sandstone Trail (ST) post confirming the way. At the hilltop keep the covered reservoir on your left and pass a National Trust sign for Bulkeley Hill Wood. The path now braids through the trees, which include some ancient sweet chestnuts that form an almost fairytale stand of gnarled old gentlemen of the woods. Behind an information board, two concrete blocks mark the top of the waterworks tramroad. Keep the steep slope to your right and trace the waymarked ST along the edge, from which are lovely views of these protected woodlands and the rich vale of the infant River Gowy below. The path gradually loses height before a series of steps drops left down to a woodland edge track.

2. Our way is left along the track (temporarily leaving the ST), from which elevated field-side route there are some grand views across the heart of Cheshire to distant Chester. Pass Grig Hill farm, bend right on the track above another house and pass Pine View Cottage's driveway to reach a sharp-left bend. Use the stile on the right here, then skirt the long field boundary on your right. Pass through the corner clump of trees to find a rough lane.

3. Go right, rejoining the ST heading west, then in 30 paces go ahead on the tree-lined path. In 50 metres use the handgate, left, remaining with the ST as an occasionally stepped way within the woods, presently reaching a great viewpoint.

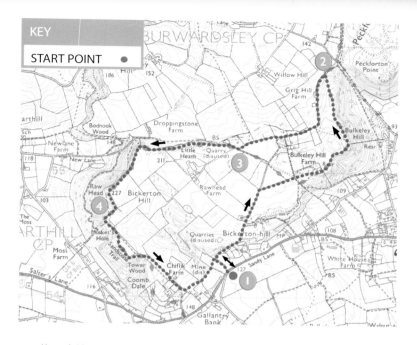

Keep faith with the ST, ignoring any paths down to the right. The path undulates to reach the triangulation pillar on Raw Head and some fabulous views to appreciate.

4. Remain on the ST, shortly descending steps. Keep left at the fork and regain some of the height lost. The path ambles along within the trees high above the deep gulch of Musket Hole (be aware of the precipitous drop on your right), eventually becoming a wide path outside the woods. Pass Chiflik Farm and advance to the right-hand bend. Here cut left onto the path

for 'Coppermine Lane', leaving the ST. It's a well-walked path which, beyond a small footbridge, passes close to the old chimneystack before reaching a lane. Turn downhill back to the start.

LYME PARK

Magnificent red deer; glorious views and a haunted woodland on a tantalising walk at the edge of The Peak District

The western fringe of The Peak District National Park tumbles down from the highest realms of the moors as a series of great fingers of gritstone, separated by deep valleys and dappled by tranquil woodlands. Lyme Park nestles in a corner of this stirring countryside; 1,300 acres of managed estate lands that surround a massive country house secluded amidst deer parks and rippling ridges which offer extraordinary views. The parkland may be managed, but it's certainly not manicured and retains a feeling of deep countryside; a hint of the wild lands that characterised these uplands a thousand years ago.

One of the National Trust's most spectacular houses, Lyme is renowned for the collection of clocks, the Mortlake tapestries, wood-carvings and the remarkable Caxton Missal – one of the rarest books in the world, printed in 1487 and in the possession of the Legh family, past owners of the Lyme estate, for nearly 500 years. More contemporary fame comes from the mansion's use as a filming location for television series like the BBC's *Pride and Prejudice* (1995) and *The Village* (2014). It's an engaging, full day out when combining a visit to the house with a walk in the glorious countryside of north-east Cheshire.

This undulating walk visits some of the less familiar parts of the parkland, an enticing mix of woodland paths, rolling ridge-top, deep valleys and reedy moorland slopes. From the main car park spread beneath stately redwood trees, the route soon forsakes estate roads for grassy paths that meander through knolly landscape where some of the magnificent red deer stags are often seen. In the rut (October) these are often solitary beasts, but for much of the year they forage together; winter is a fine time to see them, still with their huge sets of antlers, a memorable sight profiled against the skyline.

The path rises to Paddock Cottage, located on a ridge-top between two steep valleys. Its origin is probably to serve as a retreat from the hunt, where the ladies could shelter and dine whilst their menfolk pursued the deer. Enjoy marvellous views here before dropping into a deep wooded valley rich with old oaks. There's a steady, gentle climb beside the estate's fringing wall before the route gains the edge of the high moors.

It's an airy ramble now across the flank of Park Moor, where again you may see red deer grazing. The distant skyscrapers of central Manchester take the eye before the route drops through a clough prior to reaching the woodlands smothering Knights Low. Named after Sir Piers Legh, medieval knight and Lyme owner, his ghostly funeral cortège is said to haunt the wood! A fallow deer enclosure links the woods to the hall.

NB: note park opening times in the 'Basics' box

THE BASICS

Distance: 3¾ miles / 6km

Gradient: Several modest climbs, one short steep descent

Severity: Moderate

Approx. time to walk: 2½ hours

Stiles: One high ladder stile, several handgates

Map: OS Explorer OL1 (The Peak District – Dark Peak Area)

Path description: Tarred lanes, field paths, rough tracks, moorland paths

Start point: Lyme Hall (GR SJ 964823)

Parking: Lyme Hall (SK12 2NX); fee payable except National Trust members

Dog friendly: On long leads

Public toilets: Facilities in Lyme Park

Nearest refreshment: Café in old timber-yard, Lyme Park

Public transport: Buses to Lyme Park entrance, Disley (Tel: Traveline 0871 200 2233)

NB – Lyme Park Estate is open daily (not Christmas Day) 8.30am–6pm (8am–8pm from April to early October). Free entry to the parkland.

LYME PARK WALK

1. From the rear (furthest from the mansion) of the main car park turn left up the tarred road and cross the cattle grid. Just before the crest in 110 metres, bear left beside a large oak on a waymarked grassy path along the lip of a little valley. This rough pasture is often a good area  to spot some of the Park's herd of red deer. Remain on the path, which shortly passes just left of a tree-surrounded pond in an enclosure, advancing above the brook to reach a walled corner. Use the tall handgate into the woodland and then drift slightly right on the wide path, which soon curls left to follow the crest of a low ridge to find the derelict Paddock Cottage.

2. Views from here can be stunning: across Cheshire to the distant line of the Clwydian Hills in North Wales and over the gathered conurbations of Greater Manchester to the far West Pennine Moors. Beyond the cottage a wide green trod continues ahead;  walk the left-hand edge of this beside the wall. To your left is the deep gulch of Cluse Hay; the beguiling fringe of the high moors serrated by gullies and dappled by a few contorted old trees.

   In about 300 metres you'll reach a corner marked by two stunted oaks above a rocky point. Bend gently right here (not fully right on a wide grassy path) on the narrower level path, a ledged way through low birch woodland – don't drop steeply into the valley! When you reach deer-fencing in 150 metres keep left, descending past mature oaks on a path that steps down across lots of tree roots before reaching a valley-bottom track. Take care on this descent. Turn left on the track, which meanders through this fern-fronded woodland chasm to the estate boundary at West Parkgate Lodge.

3. Turn left along the lane; at the junction go left a few paces, then left up the rough lane beside Green Close Church. Keep right as waymarked at Wayside Cottage; then bear left just short of 'Lark Hill' to use a handgate. Now, walk the good path uphill beside the wall. Beyond another handgate the way passes through a wooded gulch just above a small waterfall, then steepens for a short distance as a well-waymarked grassy path up onto a shoulder of moorland. The obvious path then heads towards the distant fir plantation, here joining a rough track well right of the farm.

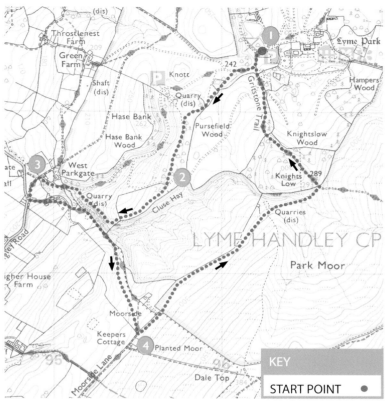

4. Turn left. At the corner in 200 metres use the high ladder stile and pick up the well-walked path, keeping the estate wall on your left. The path, occasionally rough underfoot, eventually widens to a moorland track and dips through a shallow clough before reaching the walled corner of Knightslow Wood. Use the high handgate here (waymarked Gritstone Trail) to enter the wood and trace the wide track through the trees. At one point is a marvellous view down a tree-lined avenue to Lyme Hall. At the far side of the woods turn right through the gate to return to the car park, passing the fallow deer enclosure on your right.

SADDLE OF KERRIDGE

Magnificent views from a modest gritstone ridge at the edge of the Peak District

The engaging village of Bollington ripples up the steep valley-sides of the River Dean like a giant jigsaw of the Industrial Revolution. Massive red-brick or stone, multi-level cotton mills dominate the view in some quarters; in others the spires of village churches draw the eye up to the woods which trim some of the bordering hills. Imposing transport heritage commands the heart of the place, with a bold railway viaduct striding across the Dean, whilst close by massive embankments and aqueducts chart the progress of the Macclesfield Canal through the village.

Above the terraces of houses rises Kerridge Ridge, a sharp splinter of gritstone all but separated from the rippling uplands of the Peak District's western fringe by the Dean's deep valley to the south-east of Bollington. Along this ridge a string of stone quarries has gouged huge bites from the western edge, from which a tramroad once plunged down to wharves on the canal.

All in all it's an absorbing place to explore. With its industrial history largely a memory, the village is now a desirable commuter retreat for Macclesfield and Manchester. The canal and old railway line are popular recreational routes; trendy restaurants hide down side-streets and myriad walking routes disperse into the hills and vales.

This walk links the village to the bracing walk along the thin spine of Kerridge Ridge. From a riverside park, the canal towpath is gained for a stretch, passing one of the massive old mills before breaking free of housing to emerge in pastureland rolling gently down from the hills. Lanes and paths then thread towards the uplands, leading to a steady climb up past one of the old quarries to reach the ridge at a notch cut into the Saddle of Kerridge.

Stunning views in all directions are the reward. To the west stretches the Cheshire Plain, with the dish of Jodrell Bank's radio telescope perhaps visible whilst the horizon may offer the sandstone ridge or glimpses of the Welsh Mountains or Shropshire Hills. To the east the moorland fringes of the Peak District are furrowed by deep cloughs, blistered by sharp knolls and dappled with pocket woodland amidst rolling haymeadows.

The northern snout of the ridge is capped by the oddity of White Nancy, high above the hamlet of Kerridge from which the hill takes its name. The curious, white-painted cone is a landmark from many miles around. It was built around 1820 to celebrate victory over Napoleon at Waterloo. It's said that the structure is hollow, and was used as a summerhouse by the owning Gaskell family for many years. Exhilarating views north take the breath away, as may the steep descent back to Bollington!

THE BASICS

Distance: 4 miles / 6.4km

Gradient: One lengthy moderate climb and one steep descent

Severity: Moderate

Approx. time to walk: 2½ hours

Stiles: Two, numerous easy handgates, a few steps

Map: OS Explorer 268 (Wilmslow, Macclesfield and Congleton)

Path description: Towpath, field paths, tarred lanes

Start point: Bollington (GR SJ 931781)

Parking: Adlington Road car park (free) (SK10 5JT)

Dog friendly: On leads where appropriate

Public toilets: At start

Nearest refreshment: Pubs and cafés in Bollington

SADDLE OF KERRIDGE WALK

1. Cross from the car park entrance into the recreation ground opposite and draw close to the right-hand edge above the River Dean. Cross the footbridge and go left and up the steeper stepped path to the main road. Opposite is Bollington Library; head left up Hurst Lane to the corner. Here join the towpath, with the canal on your left. The Macclesfield Canal was one of the last to be built and opened in 1831. Cotton goods, stone, lime and 'night soil' from the Manchester conurbation were the main cargoes; it's now a very popular recreational waterway.

   Remain with this for the next 1.5km. It cuts above the lower part of Bollington, passing the imposing stone facade of the immense Adelphi Mill just past an aqueduct. This was a steam-powered cotton spinning mill, opened in 1856 and working until 1974. The village is soon left behind and a rural stretch cleaves between pastures. Kerridge Boatyard, on the opposite bank, marks the wharf where a tramroad from quarries on Kerridge Hill ended. Built in about 1837, it carried stone worked into roofing slates and paving slabs to the canal. In winter you'll see a stubby chimneystack in the distant hillside trees; this vented an engine associated with the tramroad incline. Nearby stood a huge windmill, used to grind corn until about 1900.

2. At Bridge 29 the towpath changes sides. Cross the bridge, leave the towpath and remain with Clarke Lane, heading for the ridge ahead. At the sharp bend, slip through the handgate to the right of the gatehouse to Endon Hall and head left up the pasture. Two kissing gates bring you to a distant field wall in 500 metres: turn up beside it. Just before the corner use another kissing gate; go ahead on the embankment a few paces then through the handgate on your right. A field path leads to a tarred driveway above the farm, go left to reach a lane. Turn back-left up to a higher lane.

3. Cross diagonally-left, up the rougher track behind the cottage. It's a steady climb, passing close to old quarry workings. Beyond a handgate the ridge-top of Kerridge Hill is soon reached. Look left for an awkward gate/stile, then bear right along the waymarked Gritstone Trail. This is the Saddle of Kerridge, blessed by superb views. Simply remain with this undulating ridge-top through three more handgates to reach the monument of White Nancy.

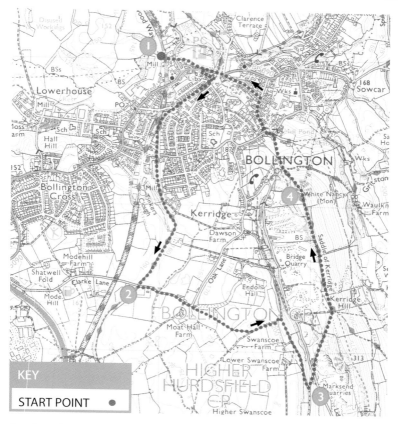

KEY

START POINT ●

4. Drop down the steep, roughly paved path. Cross directly over the farm road and choose the right-hand kissing gate. Head steeply downhill along the pasture edge; beyond a gate and steps the way becomes a paved path to a tarred lane beside the slope-foot cottages. Turn left the 60 metres to find High Street. Turn down this; in 350 metres turn left along Water Street. At the end pass under the aqueduct then enter the recreation ground. Turn left down steps then follow the riverside path to return to the start.

HELSBY HILL

DISCOVER HUMPY HILLFORTS AND WONDERFUL WOODLANDS HIGH ABOVE THE MERSEY

Like a great wave curling to crash on a shore, the sandstone cliffs above Helsby seem ready to break across the marshy pastures of the Mersey's low-lying landscape. This great wooded snout is the northern tip of the great sandstone ridge which strides down the centre of Cheshire. Woodlands crowd the steep slopes in a great arc linking Helsby and Frodsham Hills, whilst behind them a pleasant countryside dappled with farms and villages invites exploration.

This sometimes hilly ramble takes in a good mix of woodland paths and tracks, along the way finding pockets of heritage and history stretching back several millennia. Commencing from an out-of-the-way car park tucked above an old quarry, the route threads through woods to Harmer's Wood and a tranquil lane with good pastoral views across north Cheshire, before field paths and tracks progress to a lovely woodland stretch at Foxhill and Snidley Moor Wood. Parts of this are managed as an arboretum and a few side paths lead off the main woodland track. Our walk sticks with this main through-route before reaching the woodland edge at Woodhouse Hill. This is capped by the ghostly remains of one of the sandstone ridge's hillforts; undulations amidst the trees are the only visible indicator of this ancient fortification.

A steep descent down the face of the hill leads to a stretch along tracks and lanes back towards the top end of Helsby. The hillside woods here have several long-established woodland promenades; this route traces one that rises to a superb viewpoint at the summit of Helsby Hill. Set within the vague ramparts of a hillfort dating back perhaps to the Bronze Age 3,000 years ago, the panorama can include the twin cathedrals of distant Liverpool, well beyond the industrial belt that borders the Mersey's estuary stretching to Stanlow and Ellesmere Port. The line of the Clwydian Hills also draws the eye to North Wales. The walk then drops back to the old quarry car park.

From this spot a web of paths can be used to explore the area off Alvanley Road known as the Woodland Park. Details are not given here, but there are several short waymarked routes which take in the fascinating quarry remains. The stone was quarried and dressed before being moved on a horse-drawn tramroad down through the edge of Helsby and across the marshy fringe of the Mersey to a dock at Ince. From here the stone was shipped to Liverpool and Birkenhead, where it was used in many of the imposing buildings which characterise the fine architecture either side of the Mersey's famous estuary. The quarry was worked until the 1920s.

THE BASICS

Distance: 4¾ miles / 7.6km
Gradient: Several ascents and descents (one steep)
Severity: Moderate
Approx. time to walk: 2½ to 3 hours
Stiles: One, plus several lots of steps and many handgates
Map: OS Explorer 267 (Northwich and Delamere Forest)
Path description: Woodland tracks, field paths, tarred lanes
Start point: Helsby Quarry (GR SJ 491750)
Parking: Quarry car park (free) (WA6 9PT)
Dog friendly: On leads where appropriate
Public toilets: None
Nearest refreshment: Cafés and pubs in Helsby

HELSBY HILL WALK

1. Opposite the car park, head uphill on Hill Road South. Beyond houses a gap stile leads onto a woodland path. In another 150 metres fork right through a rock cutting, then ahead past Harmer's Pond, named after a local who quarried hereabouts 150 years ago. Beyond a gate the road becomes tarred Hill Road North; remain with this to the bottom end of Harmer's Wood, where a handgate, right, signed as the Sandstone Trail (ST), points the way along an enclosed path to another handgate. Bear left, field-side to a lower, derelict handgate:beyond which curl right within the strand of trees (ignore a field path,left) to a lane.

2. Turn left for 150 metres, looking for the handgate, right, onto a field-edge path. Cross a flat bridge and turn left beside the ditch to join another lane. Turn left to the T-junction. Here, go right along the quiet lane for 300 metres to a track, left, waymarked as the ST (Frodsham). Turn along this, presently entering broadleaf woods. The track rises gently for 800 metres to reach a wood-edge T-junction by pasture. Here, turn left with the ST on a good path that soon reaches a corner. Just round this and beyond the information pedestal, turn left up a lesser path into the woods. This soon crosses ditches marking the ramparts of Woodhouse Hill hillfort. The path bends right and falls to rejoin the ST; turn left to descend to a wide path at a viewpoint. Turn left on this wide path, which presently reaches another information pedestal near to a corner kissing gate.

3. Don't use the gate; rather take the occasionally stepped, steep path down through the woods to emerge onto a lane. Go down it to reach a road. Turn left, then right on Chestnut Lane. In 350 metres turn left (waymarked) in front of the cottage. The grass-centred track becomes a narrow path through to a railed footbridge into a field. Trace the left-edge along to a road. Turn right along the grassy verge. Pass Teuthill Farm; in another 150 metres turn right on Bates Lane.

4. At the bend in 150 metres use the handgate, left, and head up the pasture hollow. Cut across the next narrow pasture, then turn right on the good path (used earlier in the other direction) above the derelict hand gate back to Hill Road North. back to Hill Road North. Turn right and head downhill for 350 metres to find a waymarked lane on the left. Turn up this, which beyond Hillside Lodge becomes a dirt track. In 300 metres is a junction of paths and a stile at the woodland edge.

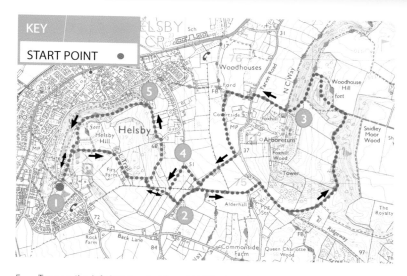

5. Turn up the left-hand path (signed Hill Top) and walk this rising way to reach the trig pillar on Helsby Hill. Views can be tremendous; a great panorama across the Mersey's estuary to Lancashire is just one treat to enjoy. The hilltop is another Iron Age hillfort believed to date from around 800 BC. Who built it remains unclear; this area was at the boundary of several British tribal territories, so members of the Cornovii, Brigantes or Decanglii tribes could have fortified the pre-existing Bronze Age enclosures here. Maintain your direction past the pillar, with the cliffs on your right. This path soon enters woodland; keep downhill to regain the car park at the foot of a tarred lane.

MACCLESFIELD FOREST

A ROLLERCOASTER ROUTE TO GREAT VIEWPOINTS, HIDDEN
HERITAGE AND ABSORBING WILDLIFE ENCOUNTERS DEEP IN A
MEDIEVAL FOREST

This is where the Cheshire Plain meets the
backbone of England. Here; the gritstone hills of
the southern Pennine Chain ripple up the edge
of Cheshire as a series of splintered fingers
of moorland, split by deep valleys where lie
secluded farms and tiny villages well away from
main roads. It's long been a land apart; in the days of the Normans it was a royal hunting
chase, protected and managed for the benefit of the monarch and his cronies who hunted
deer, wolf and boar across this wild realm.

Nowadays, it's the domain of the water-catcher and forester. The steep slopes and
valleys of these west-facing hillsides receive lots of rain that is channelled into a series
of reservoirs. The infant River Bollin is stored in woodland-fringe lakes, prior to being
supplied to Macclesfield and managed to ensure a reasonable flow for the Bollin further
downstream. One of these lakes, Trentabank, has Cheshire's largest heronry in tall fir
trees, easily seen from a viewing point passed on this walk. Both reservoirs passed
along the way are excellent for birdwatching, with water birds and woodland birds of
many species present all year round. In recent years buzzards have become increasingly
common, soaring above the woods and upland pastures.

The woodlands themselves are in a constant state of change. Great swathes of thick fir
woods have been felled in the last few years, opening up views unseen for 70 years, whilst

some marvellous stands of broadleaf forest are a delight to walk in. There are some good shows of bluebells here in late spring, but the forest is well blessed with countless wildflowers throughout the spring and summer months. The new, more spacious understorey has benefited from the loss of  firs, with countless flowers and shrubs attracting birds and insects. It's also provided more opportunity for the forest's small herds of red and roe deer to graze – they're still very timid, but early morning or evening walkers may just be lucky.

The walk starts from the shoreline of one of the reservoirs, climbing easily along lanes, then forestry roads before a lovely woodland path meanders through oak woods to reach the historic St Stephen's Chapel in the Forest. Every August an ancient rush-bearing ceremony is held here, recalling medieval days when rushes were spread on the floor to provide both warmth and fragrance against the dank damp. It's one of the few places in Britain where this is still celebrated.

Lanes then slink round, offering magnificent views of the enfolding hills, including Cheshire's highest point of Shining Tor and the distant, eye-catching peak of Shutlingsloe, 'The Cheshire Matterhorn'. From a remote parking area, woodland paths drop back to the waters in the woods.

THE BASICS

Distance: 4¾ miles / 7.6km

Gradient: Undulating with several climbs

Severity: Moderate

Approx. time to walk: 3 hours

Stiles: Two, plus intermittent easy steps

Map: OS Explorer OL24 (The Peak District – White Peak Area)

Path description: Forest tracks and paths, tarred lanes, expect mud

Start point: Ridgegate Reservoir (GR SJ 957715)

Parking: waterside pull-in at Ridgegate 500m east of Leather's Smithy pub (free) (SK11 0NE)

Dog friendly: On leads where appropriate

Public toilets: Trentabank visitor area

Nearest refreshment: Leather's Smithy pub; irregular café at Trentabank

1. From the roadside parking beside Ridgegate reservoir head west (with the lake on your left) to the Leather's Smithy pub. Here turn right up the lane, rising gradually for 550 metres, with some great views across to the distinct hill of Tegg's Nose, to reach a fork just beyond the cattle-gridded driveway. Bear left on the rougher, forestry road signed as a bridleway. At the fork in 450 metres keep left, continuing then to gain height easily through the woods. A short distance past the point another track joins from the right, you'll approach a large clearing in the forest at the boarded up barn at Hardingland.

2. Just before this building, look right for the path signed for Forest Chapel. Step over the low stile to join the decent, occasionally stepped path which climbs consistently through firwoods. In places swathes of larch have been felled, opening up grand views and allowing wildflowers to

flourish. This pine-needle-strewn path emerges into an area of old broadleaf woodland with a memorable carpet of bluebells in favoured years. Simply advance along this tranquil way, appreciating the views across the heart of Macclesfield Forest to the shapely summit of distant Shutlingsloe. The path eventually winds through an area of thicket before reaching a very rough moorland road, Charity Lane. Turn right and follow it to the hamlet of Forest Chapel.

3. St Stephen's Chapel itself is off to your left; whilst our onward route is straight ahead up the lane for Wildboarclough. The lane soon crests and bends, revealing an astonishing panorama of the deep vale of Clough Brook. On the horizon to your left, the mast and building are at Cat & Fiddle; the pub is England's second highest, at 515 metres (1,689 feet) above sea level. To its left is the very roof of Cheshire – Shining Tor at 559 metres (1,834 feet). Turn right at the T-junction and trace this lane to the Standing Stone car park.